ADVISORY COMMENTS FOR GROWTH AND PROFITABILITY
A Guide for Accountants and Consultants

Other books available in *The Practice Development Institute Series on CPA Firm Management and Marketing* . . .

CPA FIRM MERGER STRATEGIES THAT WORK

August J. Aquila, Allan D. Koltin, Marc L. Rosenberg

This first-ever detailed guide shows medium-size and smaller CPA firms how to make a carefully researched merger work the first time. The guide also includes detailed checklists in each chapter so readers can keep close account of the steps they've implemented as well as a case study illustrating a "typical" CPA firm merger, including an analysis of the productivity and profitability of the merger.
ISBN: 0–7863–0126–0

INNOVATIVE BILLING AND COLLECTION METHODS THAT WORK

Charles B. Larson and Joseph W. Larson

This unique handbook provides a step-by-step process for designing and implementing a streamlined billing and collection plan that will reduce the probability of late payments, increase revenue flow without raising fees, and cut back on bureaucracy and paperwork. Included in this handbook are all the forms needed to make the plan work and checklists to ensure that the new plan is effective and complete.
ISBN: 1–55623–032–X

THE ACCOUNTANT'S GUIDE TO LEGAL LIABILITY AND ETHICS

Marc J. Epstein and Albert D. Spalding, Jr.

This practical, easy-to-read book tells how public accountants can steer clear of liability danger. Readers will discover how to identify which areas of practice are particularly vulnerable based on previous court action and rulings, what to look for in a policy when purchasing professional liability insurance, and the foundation for developing an ethical framework that will guide accountants through dangerous waters.
ISBN: 1–55623–993–9

ADVISORY COMMENTS FOR GROWTH AND PROFITABILITY
A Guide for Accountants and Consultants

Peter F. Stone

Mark L. Frigo

IRWIN
Professional Publishing

American Institute of Certified Public Accountants/
Management of an Accounting Practice Committee

Practice Development Institute

© Richard D. Irwin, Inc., 1995
American Institute of Certified Public Accountants
Practice Development Institute

This publication is designed to provide accurate and authoritative information in regard to the subject matter covered. It is sold with the understanding that neither the author or the publisher is engaged in rendering legal, accounting, or other professional service. If legal advice or other expert assistance is required, the services of a competent professional person should be sought.

From a Declaration of Principles jointly adopted by a Committee of the American Bar Association and a Committee of Publishers.

Senior sponsoring editor: Amy Hollands Gaber
Project editor: Rebecca Dodson
Production supervisor: Pat Frederickson
Designer: Heidi J. Baughman
Compositor: Impressions, A Division of Edwards Brothers, Inc.
Typeface: 11/13 Palatino
Printer: Book Press

Library of Congress Cataloging-in-Publication Data

Stone, Peter F.
   Advisory comments for growth and profitability : a guide for
accountants and consultants / Peter F. Stone and Mark L. Frigo.
      p.   cm. — (Practice development institute series)
   Includes index.
   ISBN 0-7863-0241-0
   1. Accountants. 2. Auditors. 3. Consultants. I. Frigo, Mark L.
II. Title. III. Series: Practice development institute series on
CPA firm management and marketing.
HF5627.S76   1995   94–19477
657–dc20

Printed in the United States of America
1 2 3 4 5 6 7 8 9 0 BP 10 9 8 7 6 5 4

Acknowledgments

This book was developed from a series of articles the authors published in different accounting journals. We were encouraged to write those articles by George W. Krull Jr., National Director of Professional Development of the accounting firm of Grant Thornton. We are grateful for his reviews of those articles and for his helpful suggestions.

Peter F. Stone
Mark L. Frigo

Preface

As an auditor, accountant, or consultant, you and your firm perform a variety of activities. These include preparing reports, training, communications, administration, writing advisory comments, and serving your clients. All of these activities consume valuable resources. Some of these activities produce service features desired and valued by your clients. Others do not. Distinguishing between the two is *value analysis*. Those activities producing service features that clients desire and appreciate are *value-added* activities. If you increase resources devoted to value-added activities and reduce those devoted to other activities, you are using your resources to best advantage in a highly competitive environment. In this case, you have benefited from value analysis.

Usually, one prepares advisory comments as an adjunct to the audit. They are, in effect, a by-product. Often they are written with the same perspective as the audit is performed—as a compliance function. With this perspective, advisory comments dealing with issues other than reportable conditions are often trivial or unnecessary. The writer prepares them only because the writer believes the client expects them. When the client receives such advisory comments, he or she immediately recognizes them as trivial or unnecessary. These are non-value-added advisory comments. They are a waste of resources. They also waste an opportunity to provide clients with advisory comments that can help the client grow and improve profitability. If we apply value analysis to advisory comments, we will write advisory comments the client desires and appreciates. We will write *value-added* advisory comments.

What qualities do clients desire and value in advisory comments?

- A positive cost/benefit ratio for the client.
- Practical and effective solutions to problems.
- Client-specific and nongeneric recommendations.
- Support for the client's goals.
- Sufficient detail to be persuasive.
- Timely suggestions and recommendations.
- Easily understood advice and suggestions.

Our goal is to help you prepare value-added advisory comments with these qualities.

Peter F. Stone
Mark L. Frigo

Contents

Chapter One

What Business Advisory Comments Can Do

BUSINESS ADVISORY COMMENTS: A DEFINITION

Auditors develop suggestions to improve their clients' profitability, cash flow, and operations. These are called "business advisory comments," "client advisory comments," or "management advisory comments." These comments may also describe reportable conditions[1] as defined in professional pronouncements. Reportable conditions are identified during an audit and included in the management letter prepared as an adjunct to the audit. Relatively few of the auditors' suggestions deal with reportable conditions.

Most suggestions help the client beyond the requirements of the audit. Indeed, such suggestions add value to *any* engagement, not just audits. For our purposes, we can classify advisory comments as follows:

Advisory comments dealing with reportable conditions[1] that come to the attention of the auditor. Such comments are out-

---

1. Statement on Auditing Standards No. 60, Communication of Internal Control Structure Related Matters Noted in an Audit, defines reportable conditions as matters the auditor believes he or she should communicate to the board of directors, board of trustees, owners, or those who have engaged the auditor. These matters represent significant deficiencies of the internal control structure. These deficiencies could adversely affect the organization's ability to record, process, summarize, and report financial data consistent with the assertions of management in the financial statements.

Conditions noted by the auditor that are considered reportable should be reported, preferably in writing. If information is communicated orally, the auditor should document the communication by appropriate memoranda or notations in the working papers.

side the scope of this guide. The remaining classifications do not include reportable conditions.

Advisory comments based directly on information developed during the audit. These comments do not involve inquiry, research, or procedures beyond the scope of the audit and are covered by the audit fee. We refer to such comments as business advisory comments. The suggestions in this guide relating to the form, style, and presentation should prove helpful in preparing these business advisory comments.

Advisory comments requiring some inquiry, research, or procedures beyond the information developed during the audit. The cost of these comments may or may not be reflected in the audit fee. In some cases, comments would be developed at no charge to the client as a practice development investment. We also refer to these comments as business advisory comments. Diagnostic procedures, research procedures, and presentation suggestions in this guide should prove helpful in preparing these business advisory comments.

Advisory comments developed as a result of management advisory service (MAS) consultations or engagements as defined by MAS standards. Special fees are charged for such consultations and engagements. Comments developed in consultations and engagements are presented in reports. Diagnostic procedures, research procedures, and presentation suggestions in this guide should prove helpful in preparing these reports.

This book describes the uses of business advisory comments. It explains how to identify issues for business advisory comments and how to develop and write value-added business advisory comments.

OVERVIEW

Changes in our economy, business practices, and technology have dramatically increased competition for audit clients. These trends have altered the traditional relationship between client and auditor.

Increasingly, the auditor is assuming an additional role of business advisor. This role provides a competitive advantage by enhancing the auditor's value to the client. Business advisory comments have become a very useful tool in this expanded role of the auditor.

Advisory comments serve the purposes of practice development, practice management, and client retention. These purposes are often overlooked and their benefits lost to both the client and the auditor. This chapter surveys the many uses of advisory comments in supporting the auditor's role as business advisor.

THE INCREASING IMPORTANCE OF BUSINESS ADVISORY COMMENTS

Auditors are in the middle of a revolution fueled by a changing economy and a changing business environment. The revolution is well under way. The trends are clear. They affect the relationship of auditor and client, and they affect the significance of advisory comments within that relationship. The following are some characteristics of the revolution:

- The market for audits is more competitive and less profitable.
- Clients demand more auditor availability and shorter response time.
- There is an increasing need for consulting and advisory services.
- Accounting firms are increasing industry specialization as a competitive strategy.
- Value billing is increasing in proportion to hourly billing.
- Auditors are more involved with computers and information systems.
- Government regulation of industry, litigation, and the "expectation gap" are increasing the scope of audits.
- The skills set of auditors is expanding through training.

The market for audits is more competitive and less profitable. According to a recent survey, the single most important reason for switching auditors is fee. Twenty-nine percent of the clients who switched auditors cited fees as the reason. Clients are using every means to cut audit fees.

Many firms have lost battle after battle in fee wars. And the wars aren't over. Some firms have bought clients by charging initial audit fees below actual cost. If fees were the only competitive factor, then the market would belong to the firm that consistently charged the lowest fees.

Is there an alternative to fee wars? Differentiation is the other basis of competition. The same survey showed that 71 percent of clients switched for reasons other than fees. Service differentiates accounting firms. Fifteen percent of clients switched because of service. Business advisory comments are a key feature of client service. Truly effective value-added comments are a powerful weapon in the battle for audit client retention.

Clients demand more auditor availability and shorter response time. Another recent survey showed respondents overwhelmingly felt that timeliness was the aspect of service most needing improvement. A survey by Altschuler, Melvoin, and Glasser showed that 68 percent of middle-market clients believe major accounting firm mergers will result in less personal attention. Clients want more personal attention.

When a client sees advisory comments recommending detailed solutions to his or her specific problems, *that's* personal attention. When the auditor identifies these problems before the client identifies them and before they become emergencies, *that's* timeliness.

There is an increasing client need for consulting and advisory services. The market for consulting and advisory services is growing. Most clients can't afford in-house specialists so they buy consulting and advisory services. Who is a better source for these services than their auditors? The management letter and advisory comments are an ideal medium for offering advisory and consulting services.

Accounting firms are increasing industry specialization as a competitive strategy. Industry specialization develops logically from an effort to improve response to client needs. Both the client **and** the auditor must function in the context of the client's industry.

Preparing industry-specific advisory comments increases the value of your services in the eyes of your client and offers you a competitive advantage.

Value billing is increasing in proportion to hourly billing. Value billing is a fixed fee based on the value of services to the client. It usually produces higher fees than hourly billing. Hourly billing is the traditional basis for audit fees. Value billing is increasing as advisory and consulting services increase. Often, there are opportunities for value-billing advisory services that result from problems identified in advisory comments.

Auditors are more involved with computers and information systems. Computer consulting is the consulting service most desired by clients. The computer has reduced the need for many middle management positions as top management relies increasingly on computerized management information systems. Auditors use the computer to prepare financial statements, to conduct audit sampling, to prepare audit workpapers, and to prepare tax filings.

Special reports to the client used to require months or weeks of work. Once the client database is on the computer, the auditor can produce complex analyses and "what-if" scenarios in minutes. Computer-produced analyses, projections, and graphics are an integral part of the problem-solving process. They belong in business advisory comments.

Government regulation of industry, litigation, and the "expectation gap" are increasing the scope of audits. There is potential auditor liability in client failures to comply with increased government regulation. Illegal acts of management, product liability, and environmental pollution are examples. There has been judicial expansion of the auditors' professional legal liability. That expanded liability is due, in part, to investor expectations about the validity of financial statements, the so-called "expectation gap." These trends foster audits of increased scope. Audits of increased scope introduce new problems and a broader range of topics for advisory comments.

The skills set of auditors is expanding through training. Most states have mandated 40 hours yearly of continuing education for auditors. Ritualistic compliance with continuing-education statutes is diminishing as the need for substantive training becomes apparent. New professional pronouncements, new government regulations, and the increasing needs of clients challenge the currency of the auditors' technical knowledge. To keep up, auditors are investing an increasing proportion of their professional life in learning consulting skills, specialized industry skills, and communications skills. These are precisely the skills needed in preparing value-added advisory comments.

A New Professional Perspective

Whether a firm thrives in this revolution is an issue of professional perspective. Some auditors will follow Detroit's model. These will offer the same old services in the same old way while their practice declines. Others will adapt and merely survive. Still others possess a new professional perspective. They are proactive in developing and providing services that business needs. These are the winners. Ultimately, business advisory comments are important because the best ones are evidence of this new professional perspective.

THE MANY USES OF BUSINESS ADVISORY COMMENTS

The traditional function of the management letter is to inform the client of weaknesses in internal control structure. The trends we have just reviewed suggest a much broader function for the management letter and advisory comments: problem solving for every aspect of the client's business. Today the management letter includes comments that serve the interests of the client *and* the auditor. Let's see how advisory comments can benefit your client and support your practice development, client retention, and practice management goals. You should discover some uses you have overlooked.

Practice Development

Marketing is a pervasive motive influencing many aspects of a public accounting practice. Marketing influences advisory comments if they help you to:

- Differentiate your firm.
- Show concern for the client.
- Help clients grow.
- Sell services to existing clients.

Differentiating your firm. You may have heard of the audit as a commodity. This concept holds that audits are interchangeable like bushels of corn. If the auditor's opinion is credible, it doesn't matter who actually performs the audit. The only basis for buying an audit is price.

The concept of the audit as a commodity is flawed for several reasons. Perhaps the most important reason has to do with advisory comments. An auditor who writes value-added advisory comments is distinguishing himself or herself from competitors. This is differentiation or nonprice competition. It's as desirable in services as it is in products. Clients are increasingly sensitive to the *quality* of audit services in a service-oriented economy.

Management seldom sees any direct benefit from the audit. The users are investors, creditors, and regulatory agencies. The picture changes when we provide value-added advisory comments. Here's something that can affect cash flow and profits, suggestions management can *use*. Here's benefit for the audit fee. The auditor who makes such suggestions has a competitive advantage over the auditor who does not.

Show concern. We must show our concern for our clients. Some clients believe that we don't care. They believe that we function as financial historians and our concern for their businesses ends with the opinion letter. Too often, those clients are right.

The graph in Figure 1–1 illustrates this problem. As a financial historian, the auditor is very concerned about the client's past, only slightly concerned about the client's present, and not at all concerned about the client's future. In contrast, the client is not at all

FIGURE 1–1
Concern for the Client's Business and Timing

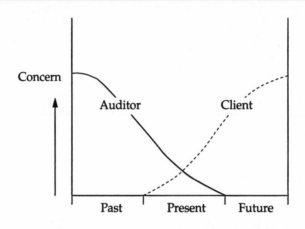

concerned about the past, only slightly concerned about the present, and very concerned about the future.

As you can see, the auditor's and the client's concerns are completely out of phase. We can bridge that time gap by showing our concern for the client's enterprise through helpful advisory comments.

It's not enough to tell the client where he or she has been. The client wants your help in reaching the destination. To help, you must take the effort to learn the client's goals. You must know where the client wants to go. The client will hire the auditor who uses advisory comments to show concern and provide a sense of direction.

Help clients grow.   Most of us would prefer larger clients. They produce larger fees more reliably. How do we get larger clients? Of course, we can target them in our practice development. There's another way. The auditor can make suggestions in advisory comments that improve the client's growth and profitability. These suggestions should produce much greater savings or earnings than they cost management to implement. They should have a positive cost/benefit ratio. Through cost-beneficial advisory comments, we help our small clients grow to medium clients and our medium clients grow to large clients.

It's not quick and easy, but it does work. And a client that you have helped to grow has much more loyalty than one bought by bid chopping, regardless of size. After all, helping the client is nothing more than enlightened self-interest. A healthy client makes a healthy practice, and a healthy practice makes a healthy auditor.

Sell services to existing clients. Many auditors overlook the chance for additional work through "cross-selling." Their behavior telegraphs the message: "I'm too busy for additional work." The client may look elsewhere for help, and the auditor loses business. The cost of additional work through cross-selling is a lot less than the cost of additional work through new clients.

When your audit client turns to another firm for additional services, that other firm is very likely to ask for the audit engagement as well. Cross-selling limits your clients' exposure to competitors: those who provide other services and who would like to provide the audit. Cross-selling is a prudent, defensive tactic.

Here is a short list of the additional services you might offer your clients:

Accounting systems design.

Acquisitions and mergers.

Budgeting.

Business planning.

Business valuation.

Cash flow studies.

Financing.

Information systems.

Inventory control.

Lease/buy studies.

Receivables management.

Tax planning.

Tax laws are constantly changing. The auditor should review those changes every year with the client's interests in mind. Certainly, you should consider any acquisition, merger, or divestiture from a tax-planning viewpoint. Inventory valuation, depreciation, equity transactions, and estate planning are often areas sensitive to changing tax regulations. Tax-saving suggestions produce a quick and tangible return that clients appreciate.

Clients may never learn that you can help with taxes, receivables management, or business planning problems unless you tell them. The management letter is a good place to do so. Hard sell is not appropriate in management letters. However, you *can* state your belief that there is a problem and that:

- Solving the problem is worthwhile for the client.
- Research is needed to define the problem and evaluate solutions.
- You have the expertise to help the client solve the problem.
- You welcome an opportunity to discuss an engagement.

Cross-selling in business advisory comments is covered in detail in Chapter 5, *Cross-Selling in Business Advisory Comments.*

Practice Management

The management letter can aid in solving practice management problems and serve some related purposes. Advisory comments may be used to:

- Improve audit cooperation.
- Defend fee adjustments.
- Highlight important issues.
- Document communications.
- Develop professional skills.

Improve audit cooperation.   Perhaps, the course of the audit can be smoothed by better cooperation between the auditor and management. During the audit, delays and inefficiencies may be due to:

- Unavailable records.
- Competing demands on client employees.
- Conflicts in work scheduling or timing.

- Poor communications between audit personnel and client personnel.

An advisory comment suggesting specific solutions to these problems could make next year's audit happier for everyone.

Defend fee adjustments. There may be situations where you can use a comment in a management letter indirectly to justify fee adjustments. Suppose your audit was over budget because the client's receivables clerk was out sick while your staff was doing fieldwork. The receivables files were in disarray, and only an inexperienced clerk was available to help the auditors. You know that the disarray of the receivables file is temporary. The clerk will return to work, or the client will hire a new one.

In an advisory comment, you describe the condition of the receivables file and the delay it caused in the audit. There is no mention of the audit fee. Give the client a chance to study the comment. You've broken the ice. Refer to the comment when you request an adjustment of the fee for additional work performed.

Highlight important issues. Use the advisory comments to show that you believe a problem is important or that you share management's concern about a problem. Suppose the CEO and members of the audit committee think the audit fee is too high. You suggest that client-prepared schedules might reduce the fee. The advisory comments may be a good place to describe the client-prepared schedules and the related savings in fees.

In the comments, you document your responsiveness to the CEO and the audit committee. By including a discussion of fee reduction, you imply that this issue is as important as any other matter in the comments. At the same time, you are emphasizing the seriousness you attach to the concerns of the CEO and the audit committee.

Document communications. Aside from weaknesses in internal control structure, the auditor may be obliged to inform management about potential or actual regulatory or legal violations. There may be conditions within the company that do not affect this year's statements but are likely to affect next year's statements; for example, a developing inventory obsolescence problem. To protect himself or herself, the auditor documents the communication of these matters to management. Advisory comments in the management letter can serve this purpose.

Develop professional skills.   No one else has the auditor's opportunity to learn about the problems of business. The management consultant is usually a specialist who reviews only a single facet of a client's business. The auditor has a wider perspective. Through the financial statements and the working papers, the auditor holds a diagnostic key to *all* facets of the client's business. Use that key and take an analytical view of your clients' operations. By doing so, you learn about the problems of business and their practical solutions.

If you have an inquiring mind and use it, each engagement increases your knowledge of business problems and workable solutions. That knowledge makes your business advisory comments increasingly valuable to the next client on the next engagement. In short, using your chance to learn increases your chance to earn.

Client Retention

As competition for the audit fee increases, retaining your present clients becomes as important as gaining new clients. Advisory comments can support this goal by helping you to:

- Improve auditability.
- Communicate with the client.
- Provide an objective view.
- Motivate change.
- Use industry expertise.
- Accentuate the positive.
- Build goodwill.

Improve auditability.   You could probably suggest many refinements for your clients' accounting systems that would increase audit efficiency. How many of these refinements truly benefit the client? How much would you cut your fee if your client carried out these refinements?

We encourage clients to make changes to improve auditability. Usually, we reward the client's cooperation by deferred fee increases, rather than by fee reductions.

By using advisory comments to persuade the client to help us improve audit efficiency, we can keep our fees competitive. By keeping our fees competitive, we're more likely to keep the client. It's a win–win proposition.

Communicate. Sometimes, the CEO circulates advisory comments to members of management. Some of these individuals are more concerned with sales and operations than with financial performance. This opens a route of communication between the auditor and other members of management who may influence the organization.

This situation presents a risk and an opportunity. The risk is that some managers may view suggestions bearing on their function as hostile criticisms. The opportunity is that these managers can be converted to powerful allies. They become allies if informed recommendations derive from a sympathetic view of the problems they face. Success depends on the auditor's command of the facts, the value of his or her suggestions, and sensitivity to the political context.

Provide objectivity. One of the strengths of the auditor is the auditor's unbiased view. The auditor *is* independent. The heat of competition and inevitable crises may distort the client's perspective. In this situation, the client may value the auditor's objective appraisal of the organization's performance. The auditor can present that appraisal in advisory comments.

Motivate change. It's discouraging to make helpful suggestions that the client ignores. When this happens, you have not persuaded the client of the benefit of following the recommendations. For some recommendations, an after-the-fact projection may dramatize the benefit. With this pro forma projection, you are answering the question, "What would have happened if this suggestion had been acted upon last year?"

For example: "If credit checks for customers had been performed last year, the cost would have been about $4,000. Based on current experience, bad-debt losses due to high-risk customers would be reduced by about $45,000. It would take $400,000 in additional sales to contribute this much to profits." Now, the CEO has a tangible motive for action. He also has some ammunition to persuade his subordinates to act.

Other steps to make your suggestions more persuasive include:

- Estimating losses or potential savings, when possible.
- Making comparisons to industry standards or ratios.
- Presenting graphs or charts to help the client visualize the problem or solution.

These and similar persuasive techniques are discussed in detail in Chapters 3 through 7.

Use industry expertise.   A survey by Services Rating Organization showed that industry expertise was the second most important criterion used by clients in initially selecting an auditor. When you write advisory comments, use your knowledge of the client's industry. It will increase your client's confidence in your firm and remind him that he has made a wise decision in choosing you as his or her auditor.

Accentuate the positive.   When a client follows a prior recommendation with favorable results, use positive reinforcement. Describe the improvements in the current comments. You will reap these advantages:

- The positive comments make the management letter seem less critical.
- Client relations are improved.
- The client is encouraged to carry out other suggestions.
- As the author of the successful recommendation, you share the reflected glory.

If the client uses your positive comment in the annual report, you've scored a triumph no matter who gets the credit.

Build goodwill. An effective people-management principle is: Praise in public and censure in private. You can use advisory comments to praise in public by citing individuals, the actions they took, and the productive results. Although the individual is named, the focus is on the action and its results. The improvement must be significant, and the description must be objective. This type of comment gives a more positive character to the management letter.

You also build goodwill by citing your sources for recommendations. Crediting a member of management for a suggestion turns that individual into an advocate. People support what they help to create.

UNWELCOME COMMENTS

Rarely, there will be situations where the client does not want advisory comments. This may occur when:

• Client management is dealing with an unsympathetic or hostile board of directors or audit committee. In this case, the auditor may try to improve relationships and reconcile differences when this is desirable and feasible.

• Management has become defensive because prior management letters were unsympathetic and too critical. Management regards the management letter as a negative report card rather than as constructive suggestions. There are specific ways of giving advisory comments a positive tone. These are discussed in Chapter 4, *Advisory Comments: The Political Context.*

• A history of impractical or insignificant suggestions in management letters has convinced management that the letter is not worthwhile. There are specific ways of getting management to "buy in" to recommendations before submitting the management letter and advisory comments. These are discussed in Chapter 4, *Advisory Comments: The Political Context.*

INTERNAL AUDITORS AND BUSINESS ADVISORY COMMENTS

Internal auditors conduct operational audits with the goals of improving operations, increasing efficiency, and identifying cost-savings opportunities. The procedures in this book for developing business advisory comments are just as useful to the internal auditor as they are to the independent auditor.

MANAGEMENT CONSULTANTS AND BUSINESS ADVISORY COMMENTS

Management consultants conduct operations reviews and other engagements with the goal of improving operational efficiency. The procedures in this book for preparing business advisory comments have direct application to this work of the management consultant and to the development of his or her reports.

IN SUMMARY

We've reviewed the many positive goals you can achieve through business advisory comments. For the auditor, improved practice development, client retention, and practice management justify the time and effort spent on advisory comments. These advantages are lost when advisory comments are rejected by the client.

Value-added business advisory comments should have a favorable cost/benefit ratio for the client. Over time, such comments will also have a favorable cost/benefit ratio for the auditor.

Chapter Two

Identifying Problems

OVERVIEW

There are many advantages to using a systematic approach in identifying problems for business advisory comments. In this chapter,
you'll review these advantages and learn four diagnostic approaches for identifying problems. After potential problems are
identified, they should be prioritized. Criteria for prioritizing problems are presented at the conclusion of this chapter.

THE USUAL APPROACH

The client sources used for advisory comments are virtually the
same as those used for an audit. There is a difference in *how* these
sources are used. When identifying problems for advisory comments, the auditor must adopt a broader perspective as he or she
notes actual or potential problems. These are the usual steps:

- Ask members of management if there are problems of
  special concern.
- Review prior management letters.
- Consider systems or procedures failures discovered as a
  result of sampling or testing.
- Evaluate adjusting journal entries and reclassifying journal
  entries as symptoms of problems.
- Review statements and accounts for significant trends or
  changes.
- Take plant tours and note observations of operations,
  procedures, or conditions.
- Review prior years' tax returns.

- Review the minutes of the board of directors meetings.
- Consider the results of analytical procedures and possibly extend those procedures.
- Prepare ratio analyses and make industry comparisons.
- Consult with internal auditors about client problems.
- Accumulate notes for the management letter in a special workpaper during the audit.

All of these steps are desirable, but they are not sufficient. Here are some of the difficulties with this typical approach to identifying problems for advisory comments:

Identifying problems is accidental.   Since there is no systematic survey, identifying problems depends on chance . . . the chance that a problem will be mentioned by management or the chance that a problem will be revealed by a systems or procedures failure. The typical diagnostic approach cannot ensure that all significant problems have been identified.

Audit focus is too narrow.   If advisory comments are merely a fortuitous spin-off of audit procedures, then much of the client's operations have been overlooked. There are too many vital business functions outside the scope of the audit. Only a broad survey can include these other business functions.

Quality control is less effective. Using the typical diagnostic approach, there is only documentation by exception. With a systematic survey, the auditor documents all the steps taken to help assure the thoroughness and quality of advisory comments.

Problems unknown to management or emerging problems are not identified.   Unsophisticated management may not recognize actual problems. Emerging problems may escape the notice of management and the auditor unless a systematic survey is performed.

Delegation is less efficient.   Subordinates need a track to run on when problem identification is delegated. The typical diagnostic approach lacks this structure. An action plan is useful in delegating specific areas for review and helps in follow-up.

A regular, structured survey of the client's business functions is clearly desirable. We'll consider four overall diagnostic approaches. These are, in effect, tools to help you identify client problems. They do not entirely overcome the disadvantages we have described. But, they *do* provide a strategy for identifying problems.

1. A review of the business strengths, weaknesses, opportunities, and threats (SWOT Analysis).
2. A rating of the value of specific business functions to the client and a rating of how well these functions are performed (Value–Performance Rating).
3. A review of the client's business functions in relation to environmental factors (Matrix Checklist).
4. A comprehensive advisory comment survey questionnaire.

There is a basic assumption in using these diagnostic tools—that you will take the time and effort to learn how the client makes money. This means you must understand:

*   The nature of the client's products or services.
*   How the client's products are manufactured or how the client's services are delivered.
*   How the client's products or services are sold and distributed.

Without this understanding, you will be unable to identify the client's problems, much less solve them.

When should you use these diagnostic tools? About two-thirds of the way through fieldwork, whether compilation, review, or audit. To use them, you must have a thorough familiarity with the client's current business situation. You will also need time while you are still in the field to investigate problems suggested by these tools . . . reviewing client records or interviewing management or staff. Remember that these tools will not always pinpoint specific problems. They are still useful if they only identify areas where problems are likely to exist.

SWOT ANALYSIS

SWOT (strengths, weaknesses, opportunities, threats) Analysis is a popular tool for strategic planning. This same tool is useful in identifying problems for advisory comments. The SWOT model has a number of advantages:

- The model is simple and easily understood by accountants, consultants, and clients. No special consulting expertise or computer skills are needed to use it.
- The model accommodates a wide variety of data: qualitative and quantitative, concrete and speculative, detailed and general.
- The model accepts the output of existing accounting and management information systems.

Here is a specific definition of the components of SWOT Analysis:

- *Strengths* are internal functions of a business that are performed well. They are effective and efficient and support growth and profitability. An example could be a distributor's fully automated and highly efficient warehousing and order-fulfillment operation. Any aspect of the business regarded as a benefit by the client's customers can be considered a strength.
- *Weaknesses* are internal functions of a business that are performed inefficiently or ineffectively. Often, these functions fail to meet standards or goals set by management. An example could be a manufacturer's rising production costs.
- *Opportunities* are external or environmental factors that give the business some real or potential competitive advantage. An example might be the opening of foreign markets for a domestic manufacturer.
- *Threats* are external or environmental factors that are real or potential competitive disadvantages for the business. An example for a plastic-pipe distributor might be proposed municipal construction regulations that reduce the use of plastic conduit.

Advisory comments tend to focus on weaknesses, opportunities, and threats for the client. But don't overlook strengths. Strengths are possibilities to congratulate management on its accomplishments in the management letter.

SWOT Analysis can be used at any stratum of detail. However, it is most productive when used to review a specific and clearly delineated function. If applied at too broad a level, analysis results in vague and useless generalizations. At the broadest level, SWOT is used to review each of these functional areas:

- Corporate/general management.
- Marketing.
- Manufacturing or operations.
- Human resources.
- Financial and management information systems (MIS).

The individual within management responsible for each of these areas should be interviewed. He or she should be questioned about strengths, weaknesses, opportunities, and threats for his or her functional area as well as for the business as a whole. In addition, workpapers and the company's accounts and statements should be reviewed from the perspective of SWOT Analysis. Once problem areas are identified, it is helpful to review the related portion of the Comprehensive Advisory Comment Survey Questionnaire in analyzing the problem.

SWOT ANALYSIS OF THE PROLAMINAR COMPANY

We'll look at a specific application of SWOT Analysis. The client was an East Coast manufacturer of industrial wood-laminating machinery with annual sales of about $11 million. The auditor on the Prolaminar Company engagement started collecting notes for advisory comments from the beginning of the audit. Three-quarters of the way through the audit, the auditor was given time during a meeting of the executive committee to raise questions for a SWOT Analysis. Here are some of the results:

Strengths

Corporate/general management. The executive committee is informed, knowledgeable, and experienced. Most members possess both operations and sales experience within the industry. The chairman of the board is the majority stockholder and a mechanical engineer. The president is a long-term employee with extensive experience in sales and engineering. The controller is a CPA who has promoted an excellent financial structure for Prolaminar. Because of the committee members' product knowledge, the company is very responsive to customer needs.

Marketing. There is a high proportion of repeat customers. These customers serve as very productive referral sources for the sales force.

Manufacturing. Superior engineering, product testing, and customer feedback have resulted in laminating machinery with a national reputation for extraordinarily high reliability and minimum maintenance.

Human resources. Prolaminar's production workers have an average experience of 12 years, a very high average for the industry. Their general skill level results in low reject and rework rates. Lower reject and rework rates help to keep product prices competitive.

Financial and MIS. For the special-machinery industry, the debt ratio is 62 percent. Prolaminar has a debt ratio of 7 percent. Considering its financial strength, Prolaminar is in an excellent position to make acquisitions or other capital investments.

Weaknesses

Corporate/general management. Decisions in important areas have been deferred too long. For instance, acquisition of land needed to expand the plant and sites for new customer service centers require approval before real-estate options expire.

Marketing. Sales staff need more technical product knowledge, particularly about high reliability and low maintenance for the company's laminating equipment. Customers are being lost to low-priced competitors. These customers have not been persuaded that their ultimate costs will be greater because of increased repairs and maintenance despite low front-end cost.

Manufacturing.   Production line machinery is old and too specialized. There is too much setup time and downtime for this machinery. The chief production engineer estimates that modern, versatile production machinery could improve capacity by 18 percent and productivity by 15 percent.

Human resources.   Management is not current in techniques for planning and budgeting. Training would be helpful in these areas. Management development is also weak. Existing management is aging, and steps should be taken to assure management succession and continuity.

Financial and MIS.   Excess cash is invested in certificates of deposit at low interest. There are other investments for excess cash that would greatly increase interest without increasing risk.

Opportunities

Corporate/general management.   There is an important opportunity for diversification. Prolaminar could acquire a product line and manufacturing machinery for hydraulic pressure applicators (power pods). These power pods are often used by Prolaminar customers along with Prolaminar's present line of wood-laminating machinery. This diversification would strengthen the competitive position of the company by assuring customers of production-line compatibility for different machines.

Marketing.   The client's equipment applies laminate adhesive by means of rollers. This is a more controlled method than the spray systems used by most competitors. Recently, OSHA and environmental agencies have stated strong concern about worker health hazards and environmental pollution due to sprayed adhesives. The concerns of these agencies represent a competitive marketing advantage for the client that has not, as yet, been exploited.

Manufacturing. If diversification is undertaken, Prolaminar would purchase manufacturing equipment for production of power pods. This manufacturing equipment is modern and versatile and could be used, in part, for the production of wood-laminating machinery. That equipment could be purchased at an approximate savings of $1.2 million.

Human resources. With the potential acquisition of the new product line (power pods), Prolaminar could hire skilled production workers from the company that presently manufactures these presses.

Financial and MIS. High interest rates have depressed the real estate market at potential sites for customer service centers. This may be an appropriate time to acquire those sites.

Threats

Corporate/general management. Prolaminar is faced with slowly increasing product-liability suits due to hazards to operators of the wood-laminating equipment. Although these suits are not an immediate threat, a trend is apparent. The company should consider such alternatives as increased product-liability insurance, operator training programs with emphasis on safety, or product redesign.

Marketing. Increasingly, wood laminates are replaced by plastic laminates for finished surfaces. Wood veneers are gradually losing market share to plastic finishes. So, research and development effort should be directed to machinery to laminate plastic film or sheets as an additional product line for Prolaminar.

Manufacturing. There is a problem of rising prices and variable quality for special-purpose alloys used in Prolaminar products. This is partly due to higher concentration and reduced competition among suppliers of the special-purpose alloys.

Human resources. Skilled machinists are difficult to find. Recruiting sources near the Prolaminar plant are less and less productive. Some long-range human-resource planning is needed to deal with this threat.

Financial and MIS. Prolaminar is located in a state with very high state corporate taxes. Presently, even higher taxes are being considered by a committee of the state senate.

As you can see, SWOT Analysis helps you build a broad picture of the client and the direction in which the client is headed. This example of the Prolaminar Company is a little unusual in that there are SWOT entries for *all* areas of the business. After completing the SWOT Analysis, the auditor would not normally investigate every problem that was identified. Instead, he or she would investigate only high-priority problems. Criteria for prioritizing problems are described at the end of this chapter.

ANOTHER SWOT PERSPECTIVE

Sometimes it's helpful to adopt a totally new perspective in identifying problems. One way to do this is to ask, "What are the strengths, weaknesses, opportunities, and threats from the viewpoint of the company's different constituencies?" By constituencies, we mean:

- Management.
- Employees.
- Investors.
- Customers.
- Suppliers.
- The public.

By viewing the company and its operations through the eyes of each of these groups as you use SWOT analysis, you may uncover problems that you would otherwise overlook.

VALUE AND PERFORMANCE RATING

The Value–Performance Rating Worksheet lists business functions. On this worksheet, each of the client's business functions is rated as to its importance or value to the client's business. Then the quality of performance of each business function is rated. Then, on the Value–Performance Grid, the business functions are entered (as key letters) according to their ratings. The location of the business function within each quadrant of the grid suggests the steps that you should take in relation to advisory comments.

Value (V). For each business and industry, some business functions will be more valuable or important than others. Each industry has an individual profile of high-value or critical functions. By value, we mean the extent to which that function contributes to the survival, profitability, and growth of the business. For instance, pricing is a critical function in most businesses and is likely to have a high value (5). In contrast, office procedures are much less critical, so this function is likely to have a low value (1).

Performance (P). Performance is a qualitative rating of each business function. How well is the business function managed and performed? Compared to other businesses, is the function performed more or less effectively and efficiently? To what extent are there opportunities for improving performance of the function? A function that is excellently performed is rated 5. A function that is poorly performed is rated 1.

Upper left quadrant (INVESTIGATE). Functions entered in the upper-left quadrant of the Value–Performance Grid have a high value to the business and are poorly performed. These functions determine whether the business will survive, show a profit, or grow. These are the functions where problems exist and where further investigation is desirable. All of these functions should be discussed with the client and some should be investigated for advisory comment.

Upper right quadrant (CONGRATULATE). Functions entered in the upper-right quadrant of the Value–Performance Grid have a high value to the business and are excellently performed. They are legitimate reasons to congratulate management. You can build goodwill by doing so in the management letter. If excellent performance results from recent management effort or from prior advisory comments, there's all the more reason to acknowledge the improvement.

Lower left quadrant (OVERLOOK).   Functions entered in the lower-left quadrant of the Value–Performance Grid have low value to the business and are poorly performed. Since these functions have low value, the fact they are poorly performed is unimportant. However, functions in the lower-left quadrant that are close to or on the line of the upper-left quadrant may be *emerging problems.* These merit some review and should be tracked. The functions in this quadrant are ignored in advisory comments.

Lower right quadrant (REALLOCATE).   Functions entered in the lower-right quadrant of the Value–Performance Grid have low value and are excellently performed. Does this excellent performance consume disproportionate resources in the form of time, money, space, materials, or management attention? Since these functions have low value, are resources misdirected? Consider reallocating these resources to high-value, poorly performed functions. After investigation, reallocating resources may be the basis of advisory comment.

VALUE AND PERFORMANCE RATING FOR POLYMORPHIC METALS

The client, Polymorphic Metals, is a Midwest manufacturer of sheet metal components on a job-lot basis for its customers. Major customers are in the electronics and office products industries. Components are manufactured by punching, cutting, bending, and assembly. Polymorphic Metals is a closely held S corporation with an annual sales volume of $30 million.

The Value–Performance Grid suggests the alternatives the auditor should consider in developing business advisory comments for Polymorphic Metals:

Value–Performance Rating Worksheet

Client: _____ Preparer: _____ Date: _____

For each business function, rate the value (V) of the function to the client on a scale from 1 (low value) to 5 (high value). Then, rate the performance (P) of each function on a scale from 1 (poorly performed) to 5 (excellently performed). Enter the letters for each function in the appropriate quadrant of the Value–Performance Grid as determined by the value and performance rating for that function.

Goals & Objectives for Mgmt.	V	P		Production & Services	V	P
GA. Mgmt. Goals & Objectives	___	___		PA. Planning & Control	___	___
GB. Short & Long Range Plnng.	___	___		PB. Purchasing	___	___
GC. Budgeting	___	___		PC. Supplier Relations	___	___
GD. Market Share	___	___		PD. Receiving	___	___
GE. Profitability	___	___		PE. Inventory Management	___	___
GF. Growth	___	___		PF. Manufacturing	___	___
GG. Continuity	___	___		PG. Quality Control	___	___
				PH. Supervision	___	___
Capital & Financial Management				PI. Mfg./Labor Cost Control	___	___
				PJ. Warehousing	___	___
CA. Equity	___	___		PK. Shipping	___	___
CB. Debt	___	___		PL. Facilities/Machinery	___	___
CC. Fixed Assets	___	___				
CD. Working Capital	___	___		**Human Resources**		
CE. Cash Management	___	___				
CF. Credit	___	___		HA. Workforce Planning	___	___
CG. Receivables	___	___		HB. Personnel Administration	___	___
CH. Billing	___	___		HC. Communication	___	___
CI. Collections	___	___		HD. Recruiting/Hiring	___	___
CJ. Accounts Payable	___	___		HE. Training	___	___
				HF. Compensation & Benefits	___	___
Organization				HG. Evaluation & Utilization	___	___
				HH. Law & Regulations	___	___
OA. Structure	___	___		HI. Industrial Relations	___	___
OB. Policy	___	___				
OC. Authority/Responsibility	___	___		**Information & Controls for Management**		
OD. Staffing	___	___				
OE. Operating Procedures	___	___		IA. General Ledger System	___	___
OF. Office Procedures	___	___		IB. Financial Statements	___	___
				IC. Mgmt. Information Systems	___	___
Marketing				ID. Data Processing	___	___
MA. Market Planning	___	___				
MB. Customers	___	___				
MC. Products/Product Planning	___	___				
MD. Pricing	___	___				
ME. Promotion & Advertising	___	___				
MF. Retailing	___	___				
MG. Sales Force	___	___				
MH. Selling Costs	___	___				
MI. Customer Service	___	___				

Value–Performance Grid

From the Value–Performance Rating Worksheet, enter the number of each business function in the quadrant determined by the rating. For example, if Continuity (GG) of Goals and Objectives for Management is exceptionally valuable to the client, but there is poor provision for such continuity in the client organization, "GG" would have a Value Rating of 5 and a Performance Rating of 1. So "GG" would be entered in the upper left quadrant.

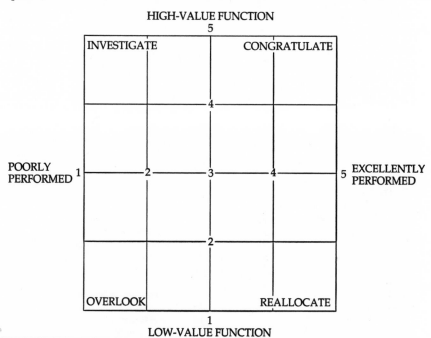

Investigate poorly performed, high-value functions as potential business advisory comments. The upper left quadrant of the Value–Performance Grid for Polymorphic Metals includes three function codes. These codes represent Inventory Management (PE), Products and Product Planning (MC), and Management Information Systems (IC). These functions are highly valuable for the company, but they are very poorly performed.

For inventory management, materials-requirements planning is very poorly performed. Overstocking has resulted in obsolescent inventory of unusable sheet-metal gauges and alloys. Lead times

Value–Performance Rating Worksheet

Client: __Polymorphic Metal__   Preparer: _____JK_____   Date: 4/3/9X

For each business function, rate the <u>value</u> (V) of the function to the client on a scale from 1 (low value) to 5 (high value). Then, rate the <u>performance</u> (P) of each function on a scale from 1 (poorly performed) to 5 (excellently performed). Enter the letters for each function in the appropriate quadrant of the Value-Performance Grid as determined by the value and performance rating for that function.

Goals & Objectives for Mgmt.	V	P
GA. Mgmt. Goals & Objectives	4	2
GB. Short & Long Range Plnng.	4	1
GC. Budgeting	2	3
GD. Market Share	4	4
GE. Profitability	3	3
GF. Growth	5	3
GG. Continuity	3	2

Capital & Financial Management	V	P
CA. Equity	2	2
CB. Debt	4	3
CC. Fixed Assets	5	3
CD. Working Capital	5	3
CE. Cash Management	4	3
CF. Credit	4	4
CG. Receivables	4	4
CH. Billing	4	4
CI. Collections	4	3
CJ. Accounts Payable	3	4

Organization	V	P
OA. Structure	3	3
OB. Policy	4	2
OC. Authority/Responsibility	4	3
OD. Staffing	4	3
OE. Operating Procedures	3	2
OF. Office Procedures	2	4

Marketing	V	P
MA. Market Planning	4	2
MB. Customers	5	4
MC. Products/Product Planning	5	2
MD. Pricing	3	3
ME. Promotion & Advertising	3	1
MF. Retailing	N/A	
MG. Sales Force	4	2
MH. Selling Costs	3	4
MI. Customer Service	5	3

Production & Services	V	P
PA. Planning & Control	3	4
PB. Purchasing	4	4
PC. Supplier Relations	4	3
PD. Receiving	3	4
PE. Inventory Management	5	2
PF. Manufacturing	5	3
PG. Quality Control	5	3
PH. Supervision	3	3
PI. Mfg./Labor Cost Control	4	3
PJ. Warehousing	4	3
PK. Shipping	3	4
PL. Facilities/Machinery	5	3

Human Resources	V	P
HA. Workforce Planning	4	2
HB. Personnel Administration	3	2
HC. Communication	2	2
HD. Recruiting/Hiring	4	1
HE. Training	4	2
HF. Compensation & Benefits	4	2
HG. Evaluation & Utilization	4	2
HH. Law & Regulations	3	1
HI. Industrial Relations	5	3

Information & Controls for Management	V	P
IA. General Ledger System	3	3
IB. Financial Statements	3	3
IC. Mgmt. Information Systems	5	2
ID. Data Processing	3	3

Value–Performance Grid

From the Value-Performance Rating Worksheet, enter the number of each business function in the quadrant determined by the rating. For example, if Continuity (GG) of Goals and Objectives for Management is exceptionally valuable to the client, but there is poor provision for such continuity in the client organization, "GG" would have a Value Rating of 5 and a Performance Rating of 1. So "GG" would be entered in the upper left quadrant.

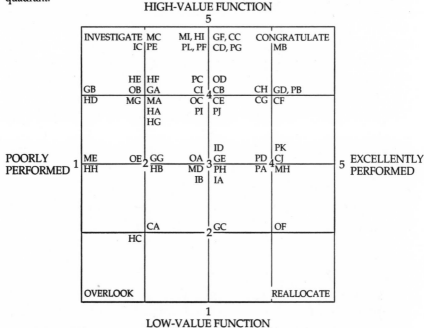

for materials orders have been too short. Inventory shortages have occurred, and these have threatened customer relationships. Sales-order data and production contracts are inadequately analyzed for inventory-forecasting purposes.

Management information systems are not sufficiently comput-erized. The problem is most acute in the area of sales. Sales trend analysis would be useful in inventory forecasting and in expanding the customer base. There is a need to analyze the profitability of specific metalworking operations to determine optimum customer or product mix. Information in all these areas could significantly improve management decisions and profitability.

Product planning is inadequate. Future growth of Polymorphic Metals will depend largely on providing those metalworking processes in greatest demand or those that can be performed most profitably in its market area. New technologies and alternative materials could threaten the present customer base. Trends in future demand should be identified and plans developed for expected tooling and staffing needs.

Reallocate resources from excellently performed, low-value functions to poorly performed, high-value functions. These are functions in the lower right quadrant. Office Procedures (OF) are excellently performed at Polymorphic, but they are of very little value to the company. Management attention should be redirected from office procedures to the functions of high value that are very poorly performed. Perhaps, a business advisory comment could help accomplish this goal.

Congratulate management for its excellent performance of high-value functions. These are functions in the upper right quadrant. Management has demonstrated excellent performance in executing two very valuable functions. These are Market Share (GD) and Purchasing (PB).

Within its market area, Polymorphic has rapidly increased its market share. This trend has been consistent despite economic downturns, increased competition, and the loss of some customers to the Sunbelt. Consistent, high-quality production at competitive prices is the reason for increased market share. It might be a good idea to explicitly recognize these achievements in business advisory comments.

Recently, management implemented procedures to improve supplier relations and reduce administrative costs per purchase. Both efforts have been successful. Arthur Green, controller, was responsible for redesigning purchasing procedures and record keeping. His contribution could be noted in an advisory comment.

Overlook low-value, poorly performed functions. These are functions in the lower left quadrant. No effort is expended on Communications (HC) within the company, but there are no evident adverse results. This function should be overlooked until it becomes more valuable to the company.

MATRIX CHECKLIST

The Matrix Checklist is used as a survey tool and a memory jogger. It is not useful for the analysis of specific problems. The checklist is based on this assumption: A business is like any living organism in that it fails or flourishes in relation to its environment. With this view, there is no absolute standard for measuring the effectiveness of a particular business function. Instead, its effectiveness depends on that function's ultimate relationship to the environment. This view is not traditional, but it has special value today because of the accelerating change in our business environment.

For example, effectively managed sales and marketing are responsive to such environmental factors as:

- Demand (affects volume of goods or services, location or siting, timing or seasonality).
- Competition and market share (affect pricing, product or service features, delivery mode, advertising).
- Customer demographics (affect pricing, product or service design, product or service distribution, advertising).
- Current economic conditions (affect pricing, distribution and selling mode, service features).
- Popular tastes and concerns (affect styling, variety, product or service features, packaging, advertising).

The key question in using the Matrix Checklist to uncover business problems is: "How well is each business function managed in relation to each environmental factor?" The Matrix Checklist is a structured approach to answering this question and thus identifying unsatisfactorily managed business functions for further analysis.

You should have a general understanding of the client's business and industry, knowledge of the results of analytical procedures, and familiarity with the client's accounts and statements before using the Matrix Checklist.

ADVISORY COMMENT MATRIX CHECKLIST

Client: _____ Date: _____

Preparer: _____

1. Add Business Functions and Environmental Factors that are important for the client and the client's industry (see listing at bottom).

2. For each cell in the matrix, ask: "How well is this Business Function managed in relation to this Environmental Factor?"

3. Enter "S" for satisfactory, "U" for unsatisfactory, or "X" for not applicable.

Environmental Factors

BUSINESS FACTORS	Present Consumers	Potential Consumers	Demand	Competition/Market Share	Technology	Suppliers	Capital Markets	Interest Rates	Growth & Inflation	Regulation	Litigation	Spending/Taxing	Popular Tastes/Concerns	Demographics	Ecology
Consumer				*Industry/Competition*			*Economy*			*Governmental/Legal*			*Social Factors*		
Marketing															
Pricing															
Advertising & Promotion						X	X	X				X			
Physical Distribution							X	X				X			
Manufacturing/Operations															
Labor Cost															
Purchasing															
Quality Control				X	X	X						X			

ADDITIONAL BUSINESS FACTORS

Human Resources
Personnel Function
Supervision
Labor Relations

Financial/MIS
Accounting System
Credit & Collections
Disbursements

Marketing
Customer Service
Marketing Mode
Order Processing
Sales Force

Mfg./Operations
Inventory Control
Mfg. Cost Control
Mfg. Process
Shipping & Receiving
Supplier Relations
Warehousing Process

Human Resources
Recruiting
Safety
Training
Wages and Benefits

Financial/MIS
Billing
Cash Management
EDP
Finance
Information Systems
Paying Accounts

ADDITIONAL ENVIRONMENTAL FACTORS

Consumer
Demographics
Public Relations

Industry/Competition
Industry Problems
Power/Fuel
Raw Materials
Transportation
Utilities

Governmental/Legal
Infrastructure–Roads/Sanitation
Public Services–Fire/Police
International Relations

Economy
Employment Level
Spending

Social Factors
Health
Education
Crime
Literacy

ADVISORY COMMENT MATRIX CHECKLIST, Continued

From the business functions rated as unsatisfactory, select those that could best be presented in business advisory comments. In selecting, consider the functions whose improvement would:

- produce the greatest increase in profitability.
- be easiest or least costly to implement.
- require the least research or analytical effort.

Management funtions selected for comment:

_____

_____

_____

_____

_____

_____

_____

Because different sets of business functions and different sets of environmental factors are important for each business, the Matrix Checklist should be tailored to the client. To do this, review the items in the Business Functions column. Then select additional business functions you believe are important to the client, and add them to the front of the matrix. Do the same with Environmental Factors.

Ask, "How well does the client manage each Business Function in relation to each applicable Environmental Factor?" The Environmental Factors are very general in character. As you consider each Environmental Factor, think of the different aspects of that factor as they may affect the Business Function. Enter an "S" for satisfactory, "U" for unsatisfactory, or "X" for not applicable in each cell. This should be a thoughtful, not automatic, process.

For each Business Function, the Applicable Environmental Factors will vary depending on the nature of the client's business or industry. Where there is no significant relationship between a Business Function and an Environmental Factor, an "X" has already been entered. If a client is involved in different lines of business, a checklist should be completed for each line of business.

For each cell that contains a "U," consider the steps that should be taken for further definition and understanding of the problem. Problems may be noted and priorities set on the back of the checklist. At this stage, you may wish to review the related portion of the Comprehensive Advisory Comment Survey Questionnaire as an aid in problem analysis. The symptoms, problems, solutions, and benefits that might be presented to the client in management advisory comments are explained in Chapter 3, *From Symptom to Benefit*.

COMPREHENSIVE BUSINESS ADVISORY COMMENT SURVEY QUESTIONNAIRE

The questionnaire (Appendix A) is organized according to the conventional sequence of business activities. There are subcategories under these business activity headings for more specific business functions. Within each business function, the questions are organized according to the process flow or information stream that is typical for that business function. Questions are also organized from the general to the specific. Here are the major business activities and subcategories of the questionnaire:

I.   Management Goals and Objectives
     A. Management Goals and Objectives
     B. Entrepreneurial Goals and Objectives
     C. Short-Range, Long-Range, and Strategic Planning
     D. Budgeting
     E. Market Share and Industry Status
     F. Markets
     G. Territories and Siting
     H. Profitability
     I. Growth
     J. Continuity
     K. Performance Measures

II. Capital and Financial Management
     A. Equity
     B. Debt
     C. Fixed Assets
     D. Working Capital
     E. Cash Management
     F. Credit
     G. Receivables
     H. Billing
     I. Collections
     J. Accounts Payable

III. Organization
     A. Structure
     B. Organization
     C. Policy
     D. Authority and Responsibility
     E. Staffing

      F. Operating Procedures

      G. Office Procedures

IV. Marketing

      A. Market Planning

      B. Customers

      C. Products and Product Planning

      D. Pricing

      E. Promotion and Advertising

      F. Retailing

      G. Sales Force

      H. Selling Costs

      I. Order Processing

      J. Servicing

V. Production and Services

      A. Planning and Control

      B. Purchasing

      C. Supplier Relations

      D. Receiving

      E. Inventory Management

      F. Manufacturing

      G. Quality Control

      H. Supervision

      I. Manufacturing and Labor Cost Control

      J. Warehousing

      K. Shipping

      L. Facilities and Machinery

VI. Human Resources

      A. Workforce Planning and Utilization

      B. Personnel Administration

      C. Communication

      D. Recruiting and Hiring

    E. Training

    F. Safety

    G. Compensation and Benefits

    H. Evaluation

    I. Law and Regulations

    J. Unions

VII. Management Information and Controls

    A. General Ledger System

    B. Financial Statements

    C. Management Information Systems (MIS)

    D. Data Processing

Many management analysts are de-emphasizing business organization (de-layering with less specialization in management functions). Instead, they focus on marketing and the consumer as the fundamental concerns that should structure all other business activities. If you or your client share this view, you may wish to begin your survey with activity IV, Marketing, and complete the sequence in detail before reviewing activities I, II, and III.

The questionnaire can be used by itself as a tool in identifying problems or it can be used for detailed inquiry into problems spotted with SWOT Analysis, Value-Performance Rating, or the Matrix Checklist. When using the questionnaire by itself, do not try to answer all of the questions. Briefly scan the questions under each subcategory to initially identify business functions with problems. After problem areas are identified, more detailed related questions should be reviewed within the particular business function. Most questions uncover symptoms rather than problems, but some questions are direct indicators of problems.

THE PRIORITY OF PROBLEMS

Time and resources are limited, and so is the client's attention span. Since you can't solve all of the client's problems, you must evaluate them and set priorities. What are the most important problems—

the ones you really want to cover in business advisory comments? The answer depends on the business context and several criteria:

Emergency.   Is there an emergency or going-concern problem that demands immediate action? Is there a high risk or threat of such an emergency? Survival or severe loss is a top priority issue. If the problem is truly grave, its solution should not be deferred for advisory comment. Immediate action *and* advisory comment may be desirable.

Large dollar amounts.   Major customers, investments, suppliers, or accounts may be affected by the problem. If the problem involves large dollar amounts, it's important to management. Even a small improvement affecting a large account can significantly benefit the client.

Major business segment or function.   Depending on the industry, some business segments or functions will have a key role while others are less important. If the problem has an important effect on a major business function (such as production for a manufacturer) or a major business segment (such as retail outlets for a retailer) it should have a high priority.

Highly profitable.   The solution to some problems can be highly profitable. Solutions to problems with a high profit potential have a high priority. Examples might be the initiation of economic order quantities for a wholesaler, automation of production for a manufacturer, or computerization for a financial institution.

Strategic key.   Your SWOT analysis may reveal a strategic opportunity or threat confronting the client. If this strategic key is clearly definable, it may deserve a high priority.

Owner's goals.   If you understand the client's goals, consider those goals in prioritizing problems. When you *and* the client agree about the importance of a problem, you can easily assign its priority.

Quick payback. The solutions to some problems offer a fairly reliable and quick payback. This is often true where tax issues are involved. Depending on your relationship with the client, you may prefer a comment on a problem with a quick payback solution to one on a more basic problem requiring a long-term solution. Providing solutions with a quick payback lends credibility to your counsel. This may earn such comments top billing in a management letter.

Easy to do. Some problems and solutions require a lot of research, others very little. For example, a queuing problem may have an elegant and easy solution that would never occur to the client. A problem that's easily solvable may deserve a higher priority.

Low priority. There may be reasons why a problem should be assigned a low priority. If you believe the solution to a problem may not be accepted or may be ineffectively implemented because it is contrary to the current corporate culture, then you may wish to defer comment until the situation changes. If the client's resources are too limited to solve the problem, you may wish to defer comment until resources become available.

IN SUMMARY

It's easy to enter unfamiliar territory in preparing advisory comments. The best protection against overconfidence is thorough knowledge of the client. We listed sources of client audit information at the beginning of this chapter. Carefully reviewing audit sources provides an essential foundation for SWOT Analysis, Value–Performance Rating, the Matrix Checklist, and the Comprehensive Survey Questionnaire. These diagnostic approaches help you evaluate the client's vital signs. They reveal only that a problem may exist. Defining the problem and developing solutions require more highly focused research. Some guidelines for this research are described in Chapter 3, *From Symptom to Benefit.*

Chapter Three

From Symptom to Benefit

OVERVIEW

Clients are most likely to accept persuasively written business advisory comments. Persuasive advisory comments have these features:

- Logical organization.
- Client-specific detail.
- Clearly stated benefits.

This chapter explains how to write advisory comments with these features. It also describes fact-gathering through interviews and includes forms used in drafting advisory comments.

THE PROBLEM WITH BOILERPLATE

We're tempted to avoid the effort and pain of solving problems by denying they exist. Business management is not exempt from this temptation. By describing a problem in vague and abstract terms, an auditor unwittingly helps the client deny the reality of the problem. A problem described in vague and abstract terms is a boilerplate advisory comment. Here's an example:

> A review of receivables shows that the system fosters slow payments and uncollectable accounts. The policies governing these matters should be changed. By tightening up these policies, the financial condition of the company could be improved.

The essence of this comment is—improve your receivables management. This recommendation probably applies to every business enterprise to some degree. It is so general that it's easy to ignore.

And that's what the client will do. Boilerplate comments produce boilerplate results. Repeating the boilerplate comment will only irritate the client, not persuade the client.

A business advisory comment should help the client *own* the problem. In the comment, the client must recognize his or her company and its customers, products or services, employees, and business trends. The client can only identify with the problem if it's specific and stated in a familiar factual context.

An effective business advisory comment must have some structure and provide a framework for the facts. This is a useful internal organization for an advisory comment:

- Symptoms.
- Problem.
- Solution.
- Benefits.

SPECIFIC SYMPTOMS

Something caused you to suspect a problem. That's the symptom. We begin with the symptom because it's a logical starting place and a diagnostic clue. It helps the client follow your reasoning. Describing the symptom increases credibility and builds a factual context for the problem.

Often you note the symptom in connection with audit procedures. Do not consider the audit significance of the symptom in the comment unless the problem relates directly to the audit.

Symptoms may consist of:

- Changes in customer accounts.
- Exceptions noted in testing or sampling.
- Observations of some condition or action.
- Remarks of a member of management or an employee.
- Financial data or trends noted in the statements.

In Chapter 2, *Identifying Problems,* you learned about the different diagnostic approaches used for business advisory comments. The symptoms you spotted by using those diagnostic approaches should be described in the initial paragraph of the advisory comment.

Here are two example symptoms from different business advisory comments:

Tailored Software

In discussing client relationships, project managers at Tailored Software mentioned friction due to billing disagreements. One manager cited a billing disagreement of $75,000 with your client, Indigo Industries. This disagreement was finally resolved in the client's favor.

Rotomotor Inc.

During our audit of Rotomotor, Inc., we examined 10 credit memos issued during the year. Nine of these credit memos were issued because of shipping errors. There were five instances in which the wrong motors were shipped and four instances in which motors were shipped to the wrong customers.

SPECIFIC PROBLEM

State the problem in concrete terms. Cut irrelevant detail, but provide enough facts for management to easily recognize its own problem. Defining the problem is a critical step because the definition often dictates the solution. Investigate the circumstances surrounding the problem. Collect information from different sources, and interview individuals with different perspectives before settling on the definition of the problem.

Here are some of the questions that may be answered in a description of the problem:

Nature of problem

- What business functions, operations, or accounts are involved?
- Who is affected by the problem—personnel, clients, customers, suppliers, stockholders?
- How are the statements affected?
- What sites or locations are affected?

- How can the real problem be distinguished from any masking problem?
- Is urgent action needed?

Scope of problem

- What is the size of the problem—how can it be measured?
- What are the costs or threats?
- How long has the problem existed—was it cited in prior management letters?
- When does the problem occur—how often?

Cause of problem

- Why is there a problem—are there multiple causes?
- Does the problem occur because something is not done at all or because something is not done well?
- Is more research needed to define the problem? If so, what kind of research?
- What will happen if the problem is not solved?

This example problem continues the advisory comment for Tailored Software:

Investigation showed that billing disagreements occur regularly. In 1989, there were 37 billing disagreements resolved in the client's favor amounting to $325,000. In 1990, there were 53 billing disagreements resolved in the client's favor. These amounted to $575,000 or 4 percent of 1990 annual billings. Without some action to reverse this trend, disputed billings are likely to increase in 1991, reducing profitability and eroding client relationships.

These disagreements result from ambiguities in contracts or failures to document client requests for additional work. Contracts are negotiated by project managers and are usually informal memoranda of agreement. Although disputes have been resolved through negotiation, these conditions are fertile ground for litigation.

This example problem continues the advisory comment for Rotomotor:

A sample of 100 entries in the Sales Returns and Allowances Account showed that 73 were due to shipping errors and all of these were rush orders. Clients are especially sensitive to the quality of service for rush orders. As a customer incentive in a highly competitive market, Roto-motor has a goal of outstanding customer service. Shipping errors conflict with this goal.

For rush orders, the salesperson phones the order to the Order Department. The Order Department clerk checks the credit standing of the customer and phones the order to Shipping. These are possible sources of error:

- Incorrect information transmitted by the salesperson.
- Misunderstanding by the Order Department clerk.
- Misunderstanding by the Shipping clerk.

SPECIFIC SOLUTION

Inquire whether solutions to the problem have been tried in the past and, if so, why those solutions were unsatisfactory. In developing a solution, look at several solutions. Consider how each solution helps or hurts (a solution may easily create new problems). Bring together the best features of each solution in your recommended solution.

Usually, there will be constraints on the solution. It may be desirable to state less obvious constraints in presenting the solution. Generally, the solution must be:

- Financially feasible and practical.
- Cost/beneficial.
- Politically reasonable.
- Consistent with the client's goals.

The level of detail you use in proposing the solution depends on the client's technical sophistication. Some clients will want to know only what should be done. Others may want to know how it should be done, when it should be done, and who should do it.

Perhaps, you can provide criteria to determine whether the problem is solved or criteria for measuring progress towards the solution. The client can be confident the problem is solved when some quantitative standard is reached . . . a certain operating ratio, for example.

Describe the advantages and disadvantages of the solution (the advantages must outweigh the disadvantages). A discussion of the disadvantages or trade-offs reassures the client as to your thoroughness and objectivity. How much does the solution cost in time and money? Will there be dislocations in service or production? What are the risks and unknowns?

Here is the solution in the Tailored Software advisory comment:

Billing disagreements could be largely avoided by requiring project managers to use a standard contract form. Project managers will sacrifice some flexibility in using standard contracts, but there are compensating benefits for Tailored Software.

Formal work order changes, including fees and client approval, should be used to record client requests for additional work. Contracts and work order changes should be reviewed and approved by the Controller and maintained in the Accounting Department. The modest administrative costs for these measures would be more than offset by savings from reduced billing disputes.

Here is the solution in the Rotomotor advisory comment:

Errors could be reduced by formalizing telephone procedures for rush orders. The person receiving the order should repeat the entire order to the person sending the order and receive confirmation of accuracy before concluding. This procedure should be required.

The persons sending and receiving phoned orders should give the highest priority to those orders in processing records. This step will assure the earliest possible discovery of errors.

A common, and major, pitfall in developing business advisory comments is recommending impractical solutions. A solution may be theoretically satisfying, flow logically from the problem definition, and still be unworkable. Even though you are not responsible for implementation, you should think through implementation to guard against an unworkable recommendation.

In one case, a recommendation to a municipality for staff reassignments promised large improvements in efficiency. The recommendation could not be implemented because of civil service regulations.

In another case, the auditor recommended scrapping certain obsolete inventory. The benefits included lower inventory carrying costs and slightly improved cash flow. After the management letter was submitted, the auditor learned that the inventory turnover report used to identify obsolete inventory had a reputation as unreliable. So, management was unwilling to take any action based on the report, and the related advisory comment was ignored.

The solution must be workable *and* management should be willing to accept it. Ways of building management commitment for the solution are discussed in Chapter 4, *Advisory Comments: The Political Context*.

SPECIFIC BENEFIT

Suppose you used the same advisory comment year after year in your management letter to Client X. Why does Client X ignore it? Because you have not persuaded Client X there's a benefit to following through with your suggestion. It's arguable that the most important part of an advisory comment is a statement of the benefit. It gives the CEO a motive to act and provides the CEO with ammunition to persuade his or her subordinates to act.

What is a benefit? It's something that the client views as valuable and desirable. Note that we're talking about the *client's* perspective and not the auditor's. A computerized ABC inventory classification system may help the auditor in his or her inventory valuation. But the benefit is not inventory valuation, it's a savings of $15,000 in inventory operating control costs.

A benefit is not only a future advantage, it may be a way of avoiding future costs or risks. Sometimes it's more persuasive to describe the financial loss or other penalty that may result if a recommendation is *not* followed.

Here are the characteristics of an effective statement of benefits in an advisory comment:

- The benefit is a logical outcome of the solution to the problem.
- The benefit is simply stated and easy for the client to grasp.
- The benefit is specific and concrete to the client.
- The benefit has been quantified where possible.
- The benefit is shown to support the client's goals when this is possible.
- The benefit is appropriately qualified.

An after-the-fact projection can highlight the benefit of some recommendations. It answers the question, "How would the situation be different if the recommendation had been carried out last year?" For example, "It would have cost about $5,000 to conduct credit checks for customers last year. Current bad-debt losses due to high-risk customers would be lowered by about $50,000. To increase profits by $50,000, $500,000 in additional sales would be needed."

Don't quantify an expected benefit unless there is a reasonable basis for projection. This is a matter of professional judgment. If such a basis exists, then the benefit should be quantified with appropriate qualification.

Be specific in describing expected results of recommendations, but include qualification. Without qualification, such statements can be interpreted as forecasts. If predicted results are not achieved and the client is disappointed, he or she may hold the auditor responsible.

Here is the statement of benefits from the Tailored Software advisory comment:

> These are the advantages of adequately documenting contracts and work changes:
>
> - Billing disputes will decrease.
> - Client relationships will improve.
> - Billing disputes that do occur are more likely to be resolved in favor of the company.
> - Exposure to litigation will be reduced.
> - Profitability will improve (suppose Tailored Software had not lost $775,000 in billing disputes in 1987).

Here is the statement of benefits from the Rotomotor advisory comment:

> For the 73 shipping errors, average shipping costs were $37. If 73 percent of the 1,500 entries in the Sales Returns and Allowance Account cost $37 each, then shipping costs for errors amount to about $40,000.
>
> There could be significant benefits in requiring salespersons, order clerks, and shipping clerks to follow the simple procedures recommended:
>
> - Reduced shipping costs of about $40,000.
> - Reduced administrative costs.
> - Greater customer satisfaction.

This structure of symptom, problem, solution, and benefit, along with other guidelines suggested in this chapter, will not apply to all business advisory comments. They may not be appropriate for comments dealing with reportable conditions. But they should be useful for most other comments. They will help you avoid a boilerplate presentation of your recommendations.

The best way of assuring that a client will accept a recommendation is tailoring it to the client's specific needs and presenting it persuasively. Is the effort justified? If you doubt it, consider the waste of the auditor's effort and the client's resources when a truly cost/beneficial recommendation is rejected.

RESEARCH TACTICS

You're familiar with the appropriate level of detail and internal organization of advisory comments. Now we'll consider some research tactics used in developing content for advisory comments. These include:

- General guidelines.
- Interviewing technique.
- Dealing with resistance.
- Help from internal auditors.

General Guidelines

Begin with an open mind. In our eagerness to be helpful and solve problems, we can rush to a problem definition and solution without sufficient inquiry. Take time to gather the facts and cross-check data. Your objectivity is a valuable strength. Don't discount new evidence because of a rigid perspective. Be ready to redefine the problem and the solution as new evidence develops.

Listen to many viewpoints. The views of those with knowledge, experience, and judgment should receive the greatest weight. But even those views can be clouded by self-interest and bias. Solicit different viewpoints. There may be disagreement on facts and their importance.

Check consistency. Use interviews, personal observations, and documentary data from inside and outside the client organization. Are those data inconsistent as they relate to the problem, or does a unified picture emerge? Inconsistency suggests more research.

Look at the context. Circumstances surrounding the problem may offer the best clues to the cause. Are there changes in the problem (quantitative or otherwise) related to its environment? What are those relationships?

Distinguish between symptom and cause. You are not seeking a cosmetic remedy. Appearances can be very deceptive. Masking problems are common. Conceptually experiment with different problem definitions to find the one that best explains all the relevant symptoms.

Interviewing Technique

As an auditor, you've frequently collected information through interviews. Usually, the data you sought were detailed and specific. Interviewing for problem solving is different. You must suspend judgment and begin with broad questions and gradually narrow your focus. Your overall objectives are much broader than they are for audit interviews. These are your objectives:

1. Gather facts with the goal of defining the problem.
2. Test facts and ideas to:
    a. Distinguish symptoms from problems.
    b. Determine importance of problem and solution to the client.
    c. Explore opinions and attitudes.
3. Generate ideas used to:
    a. Solve the problem.
    b. Define related problems.
    c. Determine and evaluate benefits.

You will want to use your own time and the interviewee's time to the best advantage. So some interview planning is needed.

Preparing the interview.   It's helpful to prepare a guide or outline for each interview based on an estimate of the interviewee's knowledge, experience, judgment, and relationship to the problem.

1. Prepare statements to introduce yourself and to describe your purpose and scope of the discussion.
2. Prepare a broad, easily answered question that introduces the subject and gets the interviewee talking.
3. Prepare key questions that throw light on the problem, solution, and benefits. These questions should progress from the general to the specific and from the simple to the complex.
4. Prepare probing questions dealing with related areas.
5. Prepare tangential questions that allow you to introduce sensitive topics.
6. Questions should be conversational, open-ended and nonthreatening.

Conducting the interview.   Remember that the interviewee knows more about the client than you do. Also, the interviewee is a potential ally in implementing the solution. Even though you have an interview guide, allow the interviewee to amplify on subjects he or she considers important and relevant. You can discourage cooperation by being too directive. During questioning, ask for facts and specific examples. Ask for access to printed data or special reports. Probe areas that you consider important. Identify relevant subjects that the interviewee is reluctant to discuss. Take notes.

One advantage of the interview is that different members of management get to know the auditor. This familiarity builds trust. With this trust, you can float trial balloons . . . tentative definitions of problem and solution. These are useful to:

- Gauge management's acceptance and willingness to change.
- Identify misconceptions and obstacles to implementation.

Find out if the interviewee can suggest additional sources or other persons you should interview. Leave the door open for an additional interview should this prove necessary. At the conclusion of the interview, thank the interviewee.

Evaluate interview results. Add detail to your notes immediately after the interview. Distinguish between facts and opinions or impressions. Note unanswered questions and areas requiring additional research. Consider these points in evaluating interview results:

- Is interview information corroborated by other data?
- Are there internal contradictions in question responses?
- What objectives of the interview were not accomplished?

Dealing with Resistance

You may find individuals who are hesitant or reluctant to answer certain questions. Why?

- In trying to define and solve a problem, you may ask about reasons for management's prior decisions or why certain conditions were not considered. These questions may imply a management failing to those individuals concerned with the problem.
- Fear of change is a common reaction. Members of management or employees may feel that investigating or solving a problem threatens their status or security.
- Resistance may be the result of experience and prudent insight as to the kinds of problems that can be solved within the present organizational context.

For the interviewer, resistance can be a valuable indicator of the changes an organization will or will not accept. The interview process itself can be a means of building trust and consensus for change. Consensus may depend on refocusing the inquiry, redefining the problem, or reformulating the solution.

Analytical ability and persuasive logic are essential, but they don't guarantee success. Members of management and employees are stakeholders in change. Successful recommendations accommodate their concerns.

The following measures have proven helpful in preventing or overcoming resistance to change:

- Include members of management who may offer resistance in the fact-finding, problem definition, and solution development processes. Preempt opposition through participation.

- Make sure interested individuals are informed of the status of problem definition and solution.
- Prepare to make trade-offs when someone's power is threatened by change.
- Develop alternative solutions rather than prescribing only one. This flexible approach avoids the dictatorial aspect of a single preferred solution.
- Present recommendations as tentative and experimental. Solutions are to be judged only on their results.
- It may be possible to structure solutions so they benefit supporters.

Help from Internal Auditors

Internal auditors often identify problems appropriate for the management letter. These may be uncovered during operational audits. Independent auditors should always consult the internal auditor and, if possible, review operational audit reports. The operations selected by management for review by internal auditors suggest management's concerns and priorities. This information is clearly valuable to the auditor in developing advisory comments.

In turn, internal auditors can review the problems identified by the independent auditor. They can help determine whether problems are important, realistically defined, and solvable. In doing so, they can protect the independent auditor from factual and political errors in identifying problems for business advisory comments.

Sometimes management is more willing to consider recommendations from the independent auditor than from their own internal auditor. The internal auditor may be "a prophet without honor in his own country." This situation complicates relations between internal and independent auditors. Internal auditors will be helpful depending on whether they view the independent auditor as an ally or an adversary. The independent auditor should build a positive relationship. These steps will help:

- Give credit to internal auditors for their suggestions.
- Support constructive findings of internal auditors.

- Since management often assigns follow-up of business advisory comments to internal auditors, recognize their concerns in framing comments.

QUANTIFYING BENEFITS

You can increase the persuasive effect of benefits by quantifying them. In some situations, it's possible to quantify benefits using one of these techniques:

- Differential cost analysis.
- Cost-of-funds analysis.
- Discounted cash-flow analysis.

Differential Cost Analysis

This approach compares potential costs for different alternatives so that the least expensive alternative can be selected. We'll use this analysis for a make-or-buy decision.

Cost to Make   **versus**   **Cost to Buy**

Variable production cost   Supplier's price

  +

Avoidable fixed cost

  +

Opportunity cost

A supplier has offered to sell helical spur gears to the client at an apparent savings over the client's manufacturing costs. In an advisory comment, we want to determine the make-or-buy cost of this helical spur gear currently manufactured by the client. In 1990, helical spur gears were produced with these costs per gear:

Variable material cost	$16.80
Variable labor cost	8.40
Overhead cost (60% fixed and 40% variable)	12.60
Total	$37.80

The client's plant has excess capacity with no alternative uses for the capacity to manufacture helical spur gears. So, there is no opportunity cost. Fixed overhead of 60 percent of $12.60 is an *un-avoidable* fixed cost. A supplier will provide these helical spur gears at a cost of $36.80 per gear.

What alternative provides the greatest cost savings per gear for the same number of gears in 1991?

It *appears* that there is a cost saving of $1.00 per gear by buying from the supplier. But, in this case, it's appropriate to compare differential costs (variable material, variable labor, and variable overhead) and the supplier's price.

Variable overhead amounts to 40 percent of $12.60, or $5.04. When this is added to variable material and labor, the total variable production cost per unit is $30.24. This is $6.56 per unit cheaper than purchase. The client will benefit in the amount of $6.56 per unit by continuing to manufacture the helical spur gear.

Cost-of-Funds Analysis

There are savings in reducing the period that funds are used for a particular purpose. Cost-of-funds analysis helps to quantify these savings or benefit. The calculation is simple:

Funds × Effective time × Annual cost of funds = Effective cost of funds

The auditor wants to show the client in an advisory comment that there can be large savings in shortening the period used to prepare debit memos. During 1990, 1,000 debit memos for about $1,000,000 were issued to vendors. Five hundred fifty debit memos for about $600,000 were issued because of rejected material and rework of vendor-supplied parts. Vendors were paid within 30 days of invoice. But it took an average of 95 days from materials rejection to debit-memo issue to process debit memos. Forty-five days would be a reasonable period in which to process debit memos. The client's incremental borrowing rate is 9 percent. How much can the client save by shortening the debit memo processing time by 50 days?

$600,000 × (50 days/360) × 9% = $7,499

This amount, less any costs of shortening processing time, would be the net benefit of following the auditor's recommendation.

Discounted Cash-Flow Analysis

Discounted cash-flow analysis is useful for quantifying benefits of recommendations that produce increased revenues or cost savings in future years. It can also be used to compare alternatives (lease/buy/make) that affect future operating cash flows to select the most economical alternative. Here is the general model:

Annual cost savings × Expected number of years ×
Present value factor = Present value of cost savings

The present value is the future cost savings or revenues, discounted to the present.

For example, a valve part is manufactured through a combination of casting and machining. Conversion to a powdered-metal production process is expected to save $100,000 per year over 10 years. We can use a financial calculator, a computer, or published tables to find the present value. The present value factor for 10 years at 10 percent interest is 6.1445. The amount of the annual savings ($100,000) multiplied by the number of years (10) multiplied by the present value factor (6.1445) equals the present value of the savings, or $610,445. The projected net benefit would be the present value of the cost savings less incremental costs of using the new process.

Let's consider a lease-or-buy example with these assumptions:

Purchase price of an overhead crane	$120,840
Lease term	5 years
Monthly lease payments	$2,750
Pre-tax discount rate	9%
Tax rate	38.4%
After-tax discount rate	5.54%

	Purchase Cash flow	Present Value Factor	Present Value Cost
Year 0	−$120,840	1.00	−$120,840
Year 1	9,280	.9475	8,790
Year 2	14,850	.8978	13,330
Year 3	8,910	.8506	7,580
Year 4	5,350	.8060	4,310
Year 5	5,350	.7637	4,080
Year 6	2,670	.7236	1,930
Total	$ 74,430	Net present value	$ 80,820

	Lease Cash Flow After Taxes	Present Value Factor (5.54%)	Present Value Cost
Year 1	$20,330	.9475	$19,260
Year 2	20,330	.8978	18,250
Year 3	20,330	.8506	17,290
Year 4	20,330	.8060	16,390
Year 5	20,330	.7637	15,530
		Present value cost	$86,720

Present value cost to lease	$ 86,720
Present value cost to buy	−80,820
Advantage to buy	$ 5,900

ADVISORY COMMENT DEVELOPMENT FORMS

The following form for developing an advisory comment should help you prepare comments with a persuasive level of detail.

BUSINESS ADVISORY COMMENT WORKSHEET

What symptoms cause you to suspect a problem exists? Be specific.

Statements and accounts: balances, changes, trends, ratios
Industry comparisons: ratio analysis
Analytical procedures: ratios, indices, trends
Observations: operations, conditions, procedures

Minutes of Directors meetings
Audit commentaries, audit evidence
Remarks by management or employees

_____
_____
_____
_____
_____
_____
_____
_____
_____
_____

What is the problem? Be specific and quantify, if possible.

What business functions, operations, or accounts are involved?
Who is affected—customers, personnel, stockholders, suppliers?
How are the statements affected?
What are any masking problems?
What sites or locations are affected?
Is urgent action needed?
How can the problem be measured?

What are the costs or threats?
How long has the problem existed?
When does the problem occur—how often?
Why is there a problem—are there multiple causes?
What research is needed to define the problem?
What will happen if the problem is not solved?

_____
_____
_____
_____
_____
_____
_____
_____
_____
_____

What is the solution of the problem? Be specific.

What should be done?	Who should do it?
How should it be done?	What are the costs or risks?
When should it be done?	Are any new problems created by the solution?

_____

_____

_____

_____

_____

_____

_____

_____

_____

_____

How will the client benefit from the solution? Be specific and quantify if possible, with appropriate qualification.

What are the savings, efficiencies, improvements?

What is the cost/benefit?

How do benefits support client goals?

How would statements or accounts look this year if solution had been implemented last year?

_____

_____

_____

_____

_____

_____

_____

_____

_____

_____

IN SUMMARY

Now you're familiar with the internal organization of management advisory comments: symptoms, problem, solution, and benefits. Specific and detailed information is needed in each area to make advisory comments useful and persuasive. You have reviewed a variety of research tactics for gathering that information.

In a perfectly logical world, your advisory comment would be evaluated solely on its merits. But businesses are social entities. To gain acceptance, the logical advisory comment must be tempered by social and political realities. This political context is the subject of Chapter 4.

Chapter Four

Advisory Comments: The Political Context

OVERVIEW

Excellent recommendations can be ignored or rejected by the client. This is likely to occur where the auditor has overlooked the political context of the problem. Factors that discourage client acceptance of business advisory comments include:

- Differing client/auditor perspectives.
- Incompatible corporate culture.
- Opposing individual or corporate goals.
- Tactless presentation of the problem or solution.

Ways of overcoming these obstacles to client acceptance of advisory comments are presented in this chapter.

AN EXAMPLE

Can a management letter go wrong? Can a politically insensitive business advisory comment sour the client/auditor relationship? Consider this case:

A long-term client experienced losses due to overspending and adverse industry trends. Over the years, two employees rose through the ranks to become officers and stockholders. Their salaries continued to rise while their responsibilities and performance diminished. In searching for ways to cut costs, the auditor computed the buyout for these officers using an established net book value formula. Their stock could be redeemed for less than one individual's salary for one year. Redemption agreements called for payment of the redemption over five years at the prime rate (less than the client's borrowing rate).

When the CEO read the advisory comment recommending the buyout, it angered him. He said the auditor didn't appreciate the former contributions and the many years of loyal service of these officers. For this CEO, these factors far outweighed the high cost of salaries.

Clearly, you may sacrifice a fair hearing and even lose the client's goodwill by ignoring the political context of your recommendations. This chapter suggests some techniques to make your advisory comments politically acceptable. It also suggests how ordinary tact can assure a more sympathetic management review of your recommendations.

NO ONE LIKES SURPRISES

In the preceding case, the auditor's advisory comment surprised the client. The client's hostile reaction surprised the auditor. It need not have been so.

The auditor prevents surprises by discussing each business advisory comment with a responsible member of management before including it in the management letter. The auditor is independent and not involved with client management on a daily basis. So he or she may lack management's detailed understanding of:

- Current plans.
- Industry conditions.
- Marketing strategies.
- Management priorities.
- Technical aspects of operations.
- Relationships within management.

Misunderstandings of these factors (and a host of others) could be a source of embarrassment to the auditor. Without informed management preview, the auditor can easily make unsound or politically unacceptable recommendations. And doing so destroys his or her credibility.

There are other advantages to discussing recommendations with management before issuing the management letter.

- Management suggestions can improve the recommendations.

- Management has notice that it will be considering the recommendations.

- Concerned members of management are more likely to support the recommendations because they have participated in developing those recommendations.

Even though you discuss your comments with members of management, don't write the comments as if management's acceptance will be automatic. Someone may read the letter who has not had a chance to discuss the comments with the auditor. You should anticipate their possible objections in the comments.

DIFFERENT PERSPECTIVES

To anticipate objections, you must look at your recommendations from the clients' viewpoint. The auditor and client may look at the same problem from different perspectives. The auditor's desire for lowered audit risk influences his or her view. The client's desire for higher profits influences his or her view. Because of these parallax views, certain polarities may occur in the auditor/client relationship.

Auditor's Concern		Client's Concern
Documentation	vs.	Cost reduction
Formalized relationships	vs.	Flexibility
Adherence to GAAP	vs.	Bottom-line emphasis
Information/data	vs.	Action
Past performance	vs.	Future growth

If you look at the same problem from these different viewpoints, you are better able to anticipate specific objections to your recommendations. Then you can counter those objections in your advisory comments. Emphasizing the client's concerns in the comments will foster acceptance, while emphasizing the auditor's concerns *may* foster opposition.

CLIENT CORPORATE CULTURE

A basic message of research in corporate culture is that culture is extraordinarily difficult to change. Culture change is *not* our goal. Here we advocate adapting to the existing corporate culture to foster acceptance of advisory comments.

In Chapter 3, *From Symptom to Benefit*, we discussed the organization and content of advisory comments. We emphasized the need for client-specific detail in advisory comments. This detail is recognition of the individuality of each client enterprise. There are obvious differences between clients:

- Large and established or small and entrepreneurial.
- Publicly held or family-owned.
- Manufacturing or service.
- Government or private.
- Differences due to industry.

These differences affect the corporate culture of specific clients. Of course, these differences must be understood by the auditor. Other aspects of client corporate culture are not so obvious. These require a greater effort of understanding by the auditor. Consider one of your own clients. How do these factors describe your client's corporate culture as evidenced by senior management?

Corporate Culture Polar Behaviors

General Behaviors

Formal communication	*or*	Informal communication
Intracompany competitiveness	*or*	Intracompany cooperation

Focus on short-term profit	*or*	Focus on long-term growth
Conservative stance	*or*	Risk taking
Team players rewarded	*or*	Superstars rewarded
Administrative constraints dominate	*or*	Productive activities dominate
Top-down management	*or*	Participative management

Decision Making

Market-oriented	*or*	Technically oriented
Fact-based	*or*	Intuitive
Quantitative	*or*	Experiential

You don't have to be an anthropologist to recognize differences in client corporate culture. You *do* need an awareness of cultural factors. It's helpful to make a thumbnail profile of your client's specific corporate culture. Then test your advisory comments and their manner of presentation against that profile to help assure acceptance. You'll be most effective if you work *within* the client's corporate culture. Let's see how the client's corporate culture might affect the form and content of advisory comments.

Decision makers have a market orientation or a technical orientation. Decision makers with a market orientation will be interested in how recommendations will increase sales, improve customer service, or provide a competitive advantage. Freeing resources for marketing investment is likely to be persuasive. Technically oriented decision makers will be interested in how recommendations will result in qualitative and quantitative improvements in the product or service. For such clients, the solution portion of the advisory comments should probably be presented in greater detail.

Communications are formal or informal. Where communications are formal, you may need more documentation for your recommendations than would be needed in an informal setting. Titles may be more important. Colloquialisms, slang, or jargon in writing will not be acceptable. Where communications are informal, a conversational writing style is preferred.

There is intracompany competitiveness or intracompany cooperation.   Awareness of intracompany competitiveness may help you anticipate and counter potential opposition to recommendations. If your advisory comments appeal to intracompany competitiveness, you should also show how benefits support overall interests of the company.

The focus is on short-term profits or the focus is on long-term growth.   If the client is focused on short-term profits, then benefits should emphasize low cost and quick payback. For this client, short-term budgeting would have greater appeal than long-term strategic planning. The reverse may be true for a client focused on long-term growth. The extent to which recommendations support strategy, goals, and mission can be most persuasive for clients focused on long-term growth.

Decision making is fact-based and quantitative or intuitive and experiential.   Where decision making is fact-based and quantitative, problem definition, solution, and benefits must be defended by careful research and hard data. If decision making is intuitive or experiential, recommendations may be made more persuasive by citing parallel experiences or prior successes of decision makers.

A conservative stance is valued or risk taking is valued. If a conservative stance is valued, advisory comments can show how recommendations protect or preserve existing assets or advantages and minimize risks or threats. Where risk taking is valued, the recommendation can be presented as an opportunity. A favorable cost/benefit ratio or payoff should be emphasized.

Team players are rewarded or superstars are rewarded. For clients valuing team players, advisory comments should recognize the contributions of others. Emphasize cooperative problem solving in developing the comments and mutual benefits. If superstars are rewarded, you may emphasize how benefits build the status of the decision maker.

Administrative constraints dominate or productive activities dominate. If administrative constraints dominate, show how recommendations support administrative policies and structures. Management is more likely to be interested in internal strengths and weaknesses than in external threats and opportunities. Where productive activities dominate, recommendations are persuasive when tied to improvements in production quantity and quality.

Management is top-down or participative. If the management style is top-down, show how benefit support the interests and goals of decision makers. Their preferred communications style should influence the way advisory comments are written. For participative managements, show how benefits support management as a group and the company as a whole. Emphasize shared responsibility and shared achievement.

Perhaps recent management literature has exaggerated the importance of corporate culture. But the concept is useful. Adapting client communications to the client's corporate culture can make those communications more understandable and more acceptable to client management. And this applies to business advisory comments.

OFFENSIVE COMMENTS AND DEFENSIVE REACTIONS

Here's a comment that lacks tact:

> Computations for estimates of warranty expense and bad debts are erroneous. Loss experience does not justify the large amounts accrued or provided. Excessive accruals or allowances could be used by management to generate misleading statements.

A comment that faults management's knowledge, competence, motives, or integrity provokes defensive reactions. The auditor must present suggestions in a way that elicits cooperation, not defensiveness. A helpful tactic is to place greater emphasis on solution and benefits than on symptom and problem. As a result, the comment has a more positive tone and constructive character.

Consider this same suggestion, presented in a positive manner:

> Amounts for accrued warranty expenses and the allowance for bad debts are too large. The following schedule summarizes loss experience and suggested provisions to anticipate such losses. By reducing the accrual and allowances to the recommended amounts, the Company would provide only for those losses that can be estimated.

MANAGEMENT LETTER AS REPORT CARD

Because of their experience with tactless or insensitive advisory comments, some managers dislike advisory comments. Comments can be especially threatening when management is dealing with an unsympathetic board of directors or audit committee. Under these circumstances, management may view the management letter as a report card rather than as helpful suggestions. The auditor should consider how directors or creditors may view the comments. Are the comments fair, or are they unduly critical?

In an attempt to be fair, some auditors present management objections to their comments in the management letter along with the recommendation. Here's an example:

> We recommend that the company review purchase orders at the corporate level to ensure that customers sales shipments are not duplicated. The order entry system could be programmed to prevent duplication of orders.
>
> Management Response:
>
> This is not a significant problem. Its origin is with customers who fail to mark 'Confirming' on documents sent to confirm telephoned orders. During the 10 months between March and December, a total of 50 duplicates were discovered from a total of 15,000 orders placed with us.

Restating management's objections may be desirable if there is a disagreement between the auditor and management on some substantive matter. In cases such as this, where the issue is not significant, there's no point in including recommendations over management's objections. The recommendation only becomes a focus of disagreement.

Consider another instance where client relations may be improved by leaving a comment out of the management letter:

The client was a closely held company that leased construction equipment. A large part of inventory included concrete molds for the grid-and-pan flooring system, a system used less and less frequently. Leasing records documented a rapid decline in the use of this system.

At the time, a complete write-off was not justified. But there was a strong probability that a complete write-off would be necessary within two years. The auditor wrote a draft advisory comment suggesting an amortized write-off of the concrete forms as obsolete. The CEO strenuously objected to the comment.

This created a dilemma for the auditor who felt she must document her advice to the CEO before the write-off became imperative. Her solution was to write a memo to the files describing the issue and her conversation, with a copy to the CEO.

In this case, there was an alternative to including a politically sensitive advisory comment in the management letter.

Some firms devote a section of the management letter to prior year's comments that have *not* been implemented. If you use this approach, inquire as to why comments have not been followed up. There may have been sound reasons for delaying action.

A review of prior comments in the current management letter can appear as a reprimand rather than as a constructive suggestion. Restatement of comments should not imply management neglect. Include additional and current information about problems, solutions, and benefits. Further emphasis of benefits is persuasive. Benefits can be quantified based on an analysis of last year's performance with the supposition that prior recommendations had been implemented. You can provide a more positive feeling in the same section by recognizing those comments that were, in fact, successfully implemented.

WHO DOES THE COMMENT HELP?

An advisory comment is most likely to succeed if it makes friends—the right friends. The benefits of the recommendation must appeal to those with the power to accept and implement the recommendation. The benefits you emphasize and the way your recommendations are written should be tempered by the answers to these questions:

How will different members of management view a recommendation?

To answer this question, you need to know how the goals of individuals oppose or reinforce each other. Although you may not have certain knowledge of individual concerns and interests, you should try to assess them.

Who has the decision-making authority for different functions or areas?

The answer to this question is complicated if the person with nominal authority does not actually exercise it.

Your recommendation has the greatest chance of success when the benefits support the goals of the individual exercising decision-making authority. There's real danger if the auditor doesn't know who actually influences decisions. Here's a case that illustrates this point:

The clients of a partner who suddenly left a CPA firm were assigned to another partner. One of these clients was a pension fund. The board of directors consisted of union representatives and management representatives from contributing companies. The companies supported the fund in proportion to their employment of union labor. The fund employed a fund administrator and retained counsel.

Using a computer program, the partner reviewed contributions to the fund. He found that the contributions to the fund of some companies had never been audited. The partner discussed this finding and his recommendations with the fund administrator. Then, the partner wrote an advisory comment recommending cycle auditing of contributions, beginning with those companies whose contributions had never been audited.

Because of his long association with the fund, the counsel had great influence with the board. Unknown to the partner, the counsel regarded himself as primary liaison between the auditor and the board. This was true even though the auditor reported to the fund administrator.

When the counsel read the management letter, he was offended. He felt that his role as liaison was deliberately ignored. He went before the Board and stated that the auditor's recommendations would only produce higher audit fees with no benefit to the fund. He said that the auditor did not merit their confidence.

If the partner had known of the counsel's influence, he would have consulted the counsel. But, because the partner was unaware of the political context of his recommendations, the firm lost the client.

Over the course of several engagements with the same client, the auditor may develop some empathy for financial managers and their problems. Perhaps the controller or financial officers were unsuccessful in persuading management of needed investment in the financial management and accounting function. When such investment is justified, a supporting advisory comment can reinforce a positive relationship with financial managers. Here's an example:

Sound economic criteria had not been used in evaluating and approving capital expenditure requests. The client's controller believed that a capital budgeting system would help to solve this problem. It would also be useful in monitoring capital expenditures. Nonfinancial members of management opposed the suggestion, believing it would unduly limit their freedom of action.

Because of the auditor's objectivity and "outside" expertise, the auditor was able to educate management. Through an advisory comment supported by discussion, he persuaded management that capital budgeting could help them optimize the uses of capital without hampering their ability to react to changing conditions. In doing so, he helped the client and made a permanent ally of the controller.

CLIENT-CENTERED COMMENTS

Business advisory comments describe symptoms, problems, solutions, and benefits ... all relating to the client. The client is the center of attention, with the auditor in the background. When comments are dominated by the pronoun "we," readers get the impression that the auditor is the star. Consider these revisions to get the client back in the spotlight:

Auditor-Centered	Client-Centered
We noted 17 customers for which ...	For 17 of your customers, ...
We reviewed the files and found that ...	Your files show that ...
We recommend raising the credit limit to $3,000 in order to ...	By raising the credit limit to $3,000, you can ...
We believe budgets are not regularly followed up.	Regular budget follow-up would improve your....

Given a choice, management usually prefers to improve profitability and cash flow rather than information systems. Your recommendations to significantly improve profitability or cash flow are the ones that grab and hold management's attention. So, in sequencing comments within the management letter, place them in order of importance to management. Place significant comments dealing with profitability up front unless there are good reasons for doing otherwise.

Use subheadings within the management letter to reinforce your message. Instead of heading the comment by account name or function, highlight the benefit. Here are some examples:

Function Subheading	Benefit Subheading
Receivables management	Reducing Receivables investment
Documenting software costs	Tax savings on software costs
Disaster recovery plan	Protecting assets
Management information systems	More useful reports

CREDITING

CEO:

Did you see that excellent comment in the management letter? It described the advantages of integrating our inventory control and traffic control systems.

Internal Auditor:

Yes! It's an idea I've been working on. The auditor picked up my suggestion from a conversation we had two months ago.

Because the auditor did not credit his or her sources, this advisory comment has negative side effects. The internal auditor feels exploited and won't be as cooperative with the auditor in the future. The CEO wonders how much of the auditor's work is original and how much is borrowed.

Positive recognition in the advisory comments is a good way to win friends and influence people. People support what they help to create. By crediting his or her sources, the auditor enlists advocates for the recommendation and gains stature as a team player. Here's an example:

During the past year, William Collins designed and implemented a budgeting and forecasting system. This system has increased control over resources and focused operational efforts on defined goals. This year's cost reduction and increase in profitability is largely due to the Company's reliance on this system.

You should be generous with acknowledgments and gratitude in the management letter. Your comments should be specific. Thank individuals for:

- Suggestions and ideas.
- Data and information.
- Help in research.

WHEN PEOPLE ARE THE PROBLEM

When client personnel are the problem, the obvious solution is to change people. Too often that solution is the wrong one. There are usually better alternatives than sacrificing experience and loyalty through personnel turnover. These alternatives include:

- Training.
- Closer supervision.
- Improved communication.
- Positive reinforcement.
- Using reference manuals.
- Redesigning procedures.

Before recommending a change of personnel, you should carefully consider these alternatives.

You may find situations where a personnel change is the only solution. Suppose there's an individual in the client's organization who is qualified by neither experience, training, understanding, nor temperament. Such an individual in a responsible position could do great damage to the client.

The auditor has several options in communicating this problem to management. If circumstances permit and the auditor believes the client will act, a confidential discussion is probably the best route. If the auditor believes documentation is desirable, a confidential and very carefully worded letter may be needed. Only as a last resort should such a matter be raised in an advisory comment.

IN SUMMARY

For management, recommendations are not compelling simply because they're included in the management letter. The auditor's recommendations face the same corporate hurdles as any other proposal. These are the hurdles of:

- Inertia.
- Fixed priorities.
- Opposing interests.
- Competing demands on resources.

By considering the political context of your recommendations, you improve your chance of boosting them over these corporate hurdles. These specific steps help assure that your advisory comments will be adopted:

- Use a client-centered writing style.
- Emphasize the ways in which recommendations support the decision maker's goals.
- Use tact in framing your recommendations.
- Deal sensitively with matters relating to client personnel.
- Anticipate objections by considering the client's viewpoint in writing comments.
- Discuss recommendations with management before placing them in the management letter.
- Consider how your comments may influence the opinions of others towards management.
- Credit your sources in the management letter.

Chapter Five

Cross-Selling in Business Advisory Comments

OVERVIEW

This chapter explores the special advantages of selling through business advisory comments. It explains how to:

- Cultivate a productive client relationship.
- Involve the client in developing a selling advisory comment.
- Include key content in a selling advisory comment.
- Follow up after the management letter is delivered.

Cross-selling in business advisory comments is an often-overlooked means of practice development. Both client and auditor can benefit from such advisory comments.

CROSS-SELLING DEFINED

The market for auditing services is saturated. Audit firms can increase their audit practices only by winning audit clients from other firms, a difficult thing to do. That's the bad news. The good news is that auditors also perform consulting services. There is an unsatisfied demand for these consulting services. Most audit firms can grow in this market by selling consulting services to their own clients.

Cross-selling is:

1. Selling consulting services to one's audit and review clients or
2. Selling audits to one's consulting clients.

There are important differences in these two selling situations.

Selling consulting services to your audit clients is relatively easy because you face minimal direct competition. It's also defensive in that it reduces your clients' exposure to competitors who are selling consulting services *and* audits. Your competitors will sell consulting services to your clients as a first step towards selling them audits.

Selling audits to your consulting clients is more difficult because, usually, you must compete directly with another firm to win the client. This requires more aggressive marketing than selling consulting services to your audit clients.

Auditors prepare advisory comments for their audit and review clients. So we'll focus on cross-selling to these clients. Why should you sell consulting services to existing clients rather than seeking new audit clients?

ADVANTAGES OF CROSS-SELLING

There are impressive advantages to selling consulting services to your audit and review clients:

- The investment in the sales process is much less than is needed to win new clients.
- The client's knowledge of the firm lowers the client's sales resistance.
- The firm's knowledge of the client often permits the firm to provide consulting services more efficiently than competitors.
- The firm may face lower risk and liability exposure because the firm knows the client.
- Selling consulting services to clients protects those clients from competitors who are selling consulting services and audits.
- Clients who benefit from consulting services have greater loyalty to the firm and are helpful referral sources.

Cross-selling through advisory comments enhances the advantages of cross-selling.

CROSS-SELLING THROUGH
ADVISORY COMMENTS

Some auditors may believe that the selling motive somehow compromises professional communications in a management letter. We're assuming that any engagement recommended in an advisory comment has an important cost/benefit for the client. The proposed engagement serves the client's true interests. With this condition, a recommendation for an engagement in the advisory comments has the same professional character as any other recommendation.

Business advisory comments can leverage your cross-selling effort in several ways.

As auditor, you have direct access to decision makers when you use an advisory comment to recommend a consulting engagement. The CEO, the CFO, other officers of the company, and directors read the management letter. You enjoy a competitive advantage in your access to these individuals through advisory comments.

You increase the credibility of a recommendation for consulting services by including it with advisory comments. Suppose you have helped the client through prior advisory comments. The client has evidence that your suggestions support his or her interests. So, the client is more likely to favor a recommendation for consulting services in the form of an advisory comment.

The client usually feels obliged to respond to advisory comments. In some selling situations, the prospective buyer may defer considering the offer for an indefinite period. The client views advisory comments as important. In most cases, the client will promptly state his or her view of a suggested engagement.

When members of management preview advisory comments, they provide input. As a result, they may "own" those comments. There's an opportunity for consultive selling when you discuss advisory comments with management before presenting them in the management letter. You can enlist management's support for consulting services during preliminary discussions of your recommendations.

Recommending consulting services in the advisory comments informs the client that those services are available. Audit firms have lost consulting business because clients didn't know that their auditor offered such services. You must be sure the client knows you are ready, willing, and able to provide consulting services.

Your special knowledge of the client is a valuable resource in identifying consulting services that benefit the client.

USING YOUR SPECIAL KNOWLEDGE OF THE CLIENT

Client knowledge. As you gain experience with a client, you develop special knowledge of the way that client operates. This is experienced knowledge. It consists of your understanding of the client's:

- Personal goals.
- Management style.
- Relationships within the company.
- Business strengths and weaknesses.

There are certain kinds of engagements where this understanding is especially valuable. Examples are succession and estate planning, finance consulting, and mergers and acquisitions consulting. Usually, the client appreciates your understanding of these matters. He or she knows that, for some services, the consultant needs information gained only through experience with the client.

For these consulting services, the auditor's experience is an important competitive advantage. The auditor can use that advantage by recommending such engagements in advisory comments. There's an additional advantage in that these engagements are valued by the client and, therefore, are not as price-sensitive as audits.

Industry knowledge. Clients value their auditors' industry knowledge. In general, your advisory comments should reflect that knowledge. An advisory comment recommending a consulting service is especially persuasive when that service has unique importance within the client's industry. For example, inventory control is a key success factor in the wholesaling industry. To serve such clients, your consulting expertise would include these types of engagements:

- Setting up Just-In-Time (JIT) inventory.
- Determining economic order quantities.
- Relating patterns in sales to inventory forecasting.

Current management concepts. Management concepts evolve with our changing economy and business conditions. Your knowledge of the client may suggest profitable and helpful applications of these current management planning and production concepts:

- Activity-based costing.
- Activity-based management.
- Computer-aided design (CAD).
- Computer-aided manufacturing (CAM).
- Computer integrated manufacturing (CIM).
- Flexible manufacturing system (FMS).
- Just-In-Time inventory (JIT).
- Material requirements planning (MRP).
- Manufacturing resource planning (MRP II).
- Optimized production technology (OPT).
- Process re-engineering.
- Statistical process control (SPC).
- Total quality control (TQC).
- Total quality management (TQM).

Business life cycle. An understanding of the business life cycle and the client's stage of business development is helpful. Use this understanding in identifying consulting services to suggest in advisory comments. It should guide you in exploring potential engagement needs. As a business matures, consulting services might well be needed in this sequence.

Business start-up

- Business plans.
- Capital sourcing.
- Forecasts and projections.

Growing business

- Financing.
- Business acquisitions.
- Management information systems (MIS).

Stable business

- Strategic planning.
- Financial controls and reporting.
- Performance and operational reviews.

Mature or declining business

- Business valuation.
- Profit-improvement studies.
- Wage and compensation studies.

Your special knowledge gives you a competitive advantage only if it's used to serve the client. Whether you can sell consulting services to an audit client depends on how you have *already* served that client.

Client–Auditor Relationship

The relationship between buyer and seller becomes increasingly important as the length and complexity of the relationship increases. Providing accounting, auditing, and consulting services is surely a more complex and lengthy process than providing most products or services. So the client–auditor relationship merits much more attention and concern than most other buyer–seller relationships.

Cross-selling occurs in the context of an existing client–auditor relationship. The character of that relationship is critical. Cross-selling is doubtful if the relationship needs mending.

The client–auditor relationship is never static. At any time, it is improving or declining. An apparently static relationship is actually deteriorating. This is true because there's no meaningful dialogue or communication in a static relationship. Continuing communication is the essence of a continuing relationship.

How do you know whether there's meaningful communication? Does the client share his or her:

- Needs, plans, goals?
- Expectations, complaints?
- Approval, appreciation?

If the client does not share these interests, it's up to you to find out why and improve the relationship. There's candor in meaningful communication by the auditor. Consider these alternatives:[1]

Improving Relationship	Declining Relationship
Makes positive phone calls	Only returns calls
Recommends	Justifies
Uses phone	Uses correspondence
Uses straightforward language	Uses "bureaucratese"
Shows appreciation	Waits for misunderstandings
Suggests service	Waits for service requests
Helps define problem	Only responds to problem
Plans for future	Talks about past
Continuously responsive	Responds only to emergency
Accepts responsibility	Blames others

---

1. This table is based on one by Theodore Levitt in his article, "After The Sale is Over . . . ," in the *Harvard Business Review* (September–October 1983).

An improving relationship is one of increasing informality. It's a *working* relationship.

We'll review a few practices that help improve relationships:

- Send news clippings about the client's business or industry if you think they'll interest the client.
- The client may send you quarterly or monthly statements or copies of minutes of directors' meetings. If so, call the client about any important items in the statements or minutes.
- Keep the client informed about progress on the engagement.
- See clients at trade association meetings and social events.
- Acknowledge birthdays and other special occasions.

Only through regular, meaningful communication can you monitor the client's level of satisfaction. Keep in touch.

You must be available and responsive. If you don't return phone calls promptly or take time to discuss the client's problems, you're sending the wrong message. You're telling the client that you're "too busy." In this case, the client will surely seek consulting services elsewhere.

Auditing and consulting are services. Mistakes *will* happen in delivering services. Clients are no different from yourself or other service recipients when there's a service shortfall. According to research by Ron Zemke and Chip Bell,[2] people with service complaints have these expectations:

1. A sincere apology for the problem (preferably delivered in person by the service provider).
2. Corrective action that's a fair remedy for the shortfall or inconvenience.
3. Treatment that shows the service provider *cares* about the problem and *wants* to provide a remedy.
4. The offer of something that atones for the inconvenience (discount, gift, or benefit).

How these expectations are met depends on the circumstances. But it's up to you to quickly resolve problems with engagements

---

2. Zemke and Bell, "Service Recovery," in *Training* (June 1990): 44–45.

and disagreements with the client. Thank the client for letting you know about them. When you resolve a client's complaint, the client has personal experience with your responsiveness. Such a client is often more loyal than clients who never complain. Firms gain most of their clients through referral. Negative PR by clients with unresolved complaints is much too costly.

Ask the client to evaluate your services. Have they been timely? Have they been responsive? How can you improve them? Use the feedback you get from the client. Then, tell the client how you have used it. With this approach, you solve problems before they become important. You'll assure the kind of relationship with the greatest cross-selling potential.

With a healthy client–auditor relationship, you can easily involve the client in preparing the comment.

CLIENT PARTICIPATION IN PREPARING THE COMMENT

Responsible members of management should preview all advisory comments. Complete this preview before including the comment in the management letter. This step is especially important for a comment suggesting an engagement. Prior discussion of the comment has these advantages:

- Management suggestions can improve the comment. The description of the problem will probably be more accurate as a result.

- With management's input, you can assure that the suggested engagement supports company and management goals.

- Involving management in preparing the comment is a form of consultive selling. The resulting comment reflects management's view of the potential consulting service. Management is more likely to request a proposal based on the comment. People support what they help to create.

Preliminary discussion is not full-bore research. You will gather information only for a brief description of the problem in the advisory comment. Here are the kinds of questions you might ask during preliminary discussion with management:

- Who can provide insight into this problem?
- How would you describe the problem?
- How can we make this engagement more valuable to the company?
- When can we perform this engagement most efficiently and productively?
- What benefits would you expect from this engagement?

With the answers to these types of questions in mind, you are ready to draft the content of the comment.

CONTENT OF A SELLING ADVISORY COMMENT

The goal of most advisory comments is to solve the client problems. The goal of a *selling* advisory comment is to gain the client's support in preparing a proposal. The selling advisory comment is much more limited in scope and detail. This is the information included in a selling advisory comment.

The problem. You must establish the fact there *is* a problem and that it merits study and solution. Present an overall description of the problem with the losses, inefficiencies, or risks posed by the problem. Describe the probable results if the client doesn't solve the problem. This description may be very useful in a future advisory comment. Explain that the problem is complex. Expertise, study, and research are needed to define the problem and recommend a solution.

The possible benefits of solving the problem. A statement of benefits is the persuasive key to a selling advisory comment. It's worthwhile to explore what we mean by benefits. A *benefit* is some value or good derived by the client from the service. It's not a quality or property of the service itself. Here we're dis-

tinguishing between a feature and a benefit. A *feature* is a property
or quality of the service that produces the benefit.

Consider your auto liability insurance. You'll never receive a
dime from the insurance. Your benefit is a sense of *security*. A safe-
driver discount is not a benefit. Low premiums are a feature. Their
benefit is your *savings* due to those low premiums. Twenty-four
hour claim service is a feature. The benefit is *convenience*. The insurance company has been in business for 100 years. That's a feature. The benefit is your *confidence* the company will be there when
you need it.

It's a matter of emphasis. That emphasis is on what the consumer
(client) actually values and desires. In selling services, accounting
firms usually amplify features and overlook benefits. This is boast-
ing rather than appealing to the client's interests. Here's a partial
list of benefits you can emphasize:

Greater profits
Lowered costs
Greater sales
Higher productivity
Improved efficiency
Greater effectiveness
More usefulness
Greater security
Improved control
More timeliness
Greater credibility
More accuracy
More thoroughness
More reliability
Improved relations
Lowered risk
Improved responsiveness

Describe the benefits the client may receive by solving the problem. These benefits should support company goals and appeal to
decision makers. They should be logical outcomes of solving the
problem. State your belief that solving the problem has a significant

cost/benefit ratio for the client. Appropriate qualification is important in describing benefits. Point out that actual benefits depend on the problem definition and proposed solution. These, in turn, depend on study and research conducted during the engagement, as well as management implementation.

Benefits were discussed in Chapter 3, *From Symptom to Benefit.* Those guidelines apply as well to cross-selling in advisory comments.

Your consulting expertise. Briefly state your qualifications for conducting the engagement. These might include similar consulting engagements for similar clients, industry knowledge, special experience of staff members, and so on.

State your desire to submit a proposal. The proposal is the goal of this advisory comment. You must let the client know that you *want* to perform this engagement.

Now let's look at an example selling advisory comment.

AN EXAMPLE SELLING ADVISORY COMMENT

Improving Profitability

Viva's increase in sales from $230 million in 1988 to $282 million in 1993 is an outstanding achievement. The increase in sales continues a trend due, in part, to Viva's introduction of new products. In the last five years, Viva has expanded its product line of valves to include meters and hydraulic servomechanisms.

Recently the value of increased sales for Viva has been greatly decreased by the rising cost of sales (the sum of direct costs, direct labor, and manufacturing overhead). The rising cost of sales has eroded profitability. Gross profit (sales less cost of sales) has declined from 34 percent in 1988 to 18 percent in 1993. The trend suggests that gross profit will decrease even more rapidly. Without some corrective measures, there's likely to be a decline of gross profit to 10 percent in 1994.

Here is a graph of the five-year relationship between sales and cost of sales. Rapidly decreasing gross profit is clear as cost of sales rises to the sales curve.

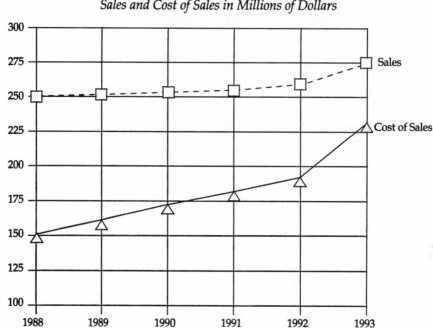

Viva Valve Company
Sales and Cost of Sales in Millions of Dollars

Viva's present accounting system provides some cost accounting information. But that information is not sufficiently detailed or properly organized to guide management's decisions. Management needs analytical cost accounting data to improve profitability. Reports from a comprehensive cost accounting system would provide this data.

Management can use cost accounting data to determine each product line's contribution to gross profit. This information is vital in pricing decisions. Management can use cost accounting data to control costs through continuous comparisons of actual costs to budgets and standard costs.

Cost accounting information can guide other business decisions. For example, in 1993 Viva spent $860,000 for equipment to modernize production of its variable-flow meter. What does the variable-flow meter actually cost in comparison to the constant-flow meter? How much do either of these meters contribute to profitability? Answers to these and similar questions help you evaluate fixed-asset investments.

The major benefit of a cost accounting system is that it would enable Viva to identify its most profitable product lines. Then, Viva could focus resources to support those lines. Viva could also identify unprofitable product lines and make them more profitable or drop them. Both measures contribute to gross profit.

Actual improvement in gross profit depends on study results, design, and implementation of the cost accounting system. Designing the system requires a research and development effort and expertise in manufacturing cost accounting.

Our Firm has expertise and experience in developing cost accounting systems for manufacturers. We believe that a cost accounting system would significantly benefit Viva Valve. We welcome an opportunity to discuss such an engagement. At your request, we will be happy to prepare a proposal to develop a cost accounting system.

FOLLOW-UP

Follow-up begins when the client has received and distributed the management letter. Talk to the person who makes the buying decisions. Present any additional information about the problem or engagement. Also describe any time constraints. Engagement results may have greater value before some deadline or report date. Perhaps you could more efficiently perform the engagement within some time bracket.

If the client declines to consider a proposal or rejects the proposal, continue to track the problem. You have already described the results if the problem were to remain unsolved. In time, events may confirm your predictions. In this case, you have very persuasive evidence for a selling advisory comment in the next management letter.

If the client agrees to consider a proposal, then it is developed through needs identification and consultation with management.

PROPOSAL CONTENT

Usually, a proposal includes these items of information:

1. Description of the client's needs, problem, or concerns. If possible, this description should use the same words used by the client.
2. A statement of benefits. All of the guidelines previously discussed should be used in the statement of benefits, with appropriate qualification.
3. Implementation. A description of what work is to be done, how it is to be done, when it is to be done, and who will do it. In other words, a work plan specifying what the auditor will do and what the client will do.
4. Engagement product. The nature of the report to be delivered by the auditor should be described. This is essential to avoid misunderstandings or to avoid false expectations.
5. Timing and fees. A schedule for completion, along with benchmarks for measuring work progress. Billing arrangements and fees are clearly detailed. Procedures for changes in the nature or scope of the work are described.
6. Request for authorization and acknowledgment of understanding. This portion of the proposal may be referred to as an engagement letter.
7. Additional information. This may include the firm's related work experience, data on the firm's capabilities, staff biographies, and so on.

In reviewing the proposal, the client is likely to consider it as an indicator of the quality of your firm's engagement product.

PRESENTING THE PROPOSAL

The proposal is usually presented orally before it's presented as a document. Like an advisory comment, it should contain no surprises. During oral presentation, you can evaluate the client's reactions and provide explanations and proposal adjustments as needed. Make sure you have a specific time commitment for the presentation. Stay within that time allocation, allowing ample time for questions and discussion.

Your presentation should be planned and rehearsed. The goal is to have the client sign, or verbally agree to sign, the engagement letter at the time of presentation. Here are the steps in the presentation:

- Prepare an agenda for the meeting and briefly review it.
- Describe the client's needs, using the client's words as much as possible.
- Ask whether these are still the needs and whether they have been correctly described.
- Describe your experience with similar engagements and your special capabilities.
- Explain how you will satisfy the need or solve the client's problem.
- State the benefits the client will receive from your services.
- Ask for any questions. In preparation, you have thought up the toughest possible questions or objections the client could raise and you have prepared your answers.
- After all questions have been answered, ask whether your proposal satisfies their need.
- Deliver the proposal.
- To close, ask one of these questions:
  - When can we begin work?
  - Would you authorize our engagement letter?
  - When can we expect your approval of the proposal?

REASSURING THE CLIENT

If the client accepts your proposal, your need to communicate has increased, not decreased. Usually, the client has doubts about the engagement after he or she has committed to it:

- Was this a wise move?
- Will the auditor perform as promised?
- Could I have gotten the same service at a lower fee?
- Will the work be completed on schedule?

These post-commitment anxieties are best allayed through close communication.

IN SUMMARY

The auditor is increasingly a business adviser. To serve the client in this role, the auditor must acquire consulting skills. Investment in these skills motivates a search for opportunities to use them. Cross-selling through advisory comments is a practical way of developing these opportunities.

We have reviewed essential steps in cross-selling through advisory comments. These include:

- Identifying potential engagements by using the auditor's special knowledge of the client's business, industry, and stage of development.
- Fostering a positive client–auditor relationship as a basis for future engagements.
- Involving the client in developing selling advisory comments.
- Presenting key content in the advisory comment.
- Taking the necessary follow-up steps to secure an engagement.

Although this approach should be productive, it does not overcome a basic limitation of selling through advisory comments. Advisory comments are usually prepared as a reaction to problems rather than as the result of systematic diagnosis. An alternative may be a formal supplement to the attest function. The future may find the auditor conducting a regular diagnostic survey to uncover client needs. Such surveys would be cost-efficient engagements in themselves. Cross-selling and consulting engagements could be a mutually beneficial outcome of these surveys.

Chapter Six

Help from the Microcomputer

OVERVIEW

The microcomputer is a tool ideally suited for the work of accountants, auditors, and consultants. Surprisingly, it is underutilized. Studies show that analysis and database applications are distant runners up to word processing and spreadsheet applications. Certainly, analysis and database applications are key functions in developing advisory comments. Our goal is more important than maximizing the return on your investment in computing hardware and software. It is to use the microcomputer creatively to identify and solve your clients' problems. In this chapter, you'll learn how microcomputers can help you meet and exceed your clients' expectations.

WHAT CLIENTS EXPECT

Clients expect auditors and consultants to be as knowledgeable as themselves in computer applications. They expect familiarity with generic software such as word processors, spreadsheets, and databases. They also expect some knowledge of the uses of computers within their industry. What are the industry-specific computer applications for your clients? For a retailing chain, the application might be on-line ordering and restocking from suppliers. For a trucking or transportation company, the application might be optimized routing software.

Clients expect a short response time. Speed is the preeminent virtue of computers. Financial statements and projections that used to require weeks of work now take only hours or minutes. Revisions take only seconds. Clients appreciate a short response time whether or not a management decision is pending. If you can access a client database on your own computer, you can anticipate the client's decision support needs and exceed the client's expectations.

Clients expect a professional finish for the report. Word processors and graphics capabilities provide that finish. With the microcomputer, small firms can produce reports with a professional appearance that no large firm can improve upon. Graphs are a standard feature of current word processing software. With the graph function, you can easily illustrate complex relationships. Graphs dramatize your message for the client and lend polish to the final report.

Clients expect useful results. Recommendations based on the client's own data are more likely to be valid and useful than generic or academic recommendations. The microcomputer has tremendous diagnostic power. With it, you can perform a CAT scan of the client's database and then address specific solutions to specific problems. Here is a list of a few of the computerized services you can perform for clients:

Amortization schedules
Bank loan assessment
Budgeting
Cash flow analysis
Contribution margin analysis
Cost–volume–profit analysis
Flowcharting
Internal rate of return
Inventory valuation
Lease calculations
Merger and acquisition analysis
Personal financial planning
Present-value calculation
Projections
Ratio analysis
Regression correlation

Sensitivity analysis

System modeling

Trend analysis

For many of these applications, you must access the client's database.

THE CLIENT'S DATABASE

The hard disk capacities and random access memories of microcomputers have increased dramatically in recent years. This increased power permits you to process data files from virtually all small and midsized clients on the microcomputer. There are a number of software programs that permit you to import data files from a great many software sources. An example is IDEA (Interactive Data Extraction and Analysis) software developed by the Canadian Institute of Chartered Accountants. The data file types that you can import include dBASE, ASCIII, EBCDIC, Lotus, BASIC and all of the major accounting software packages. Once imported, the diagnostic operations you can perform are truly impressive. Here is a partial listing:

Select records. Set up criteria to select records from the file based on quantities, dates, names, and so on, depending on the format (fields) of the records. You can use any combination of criteria as well.

Sampling. Sample records on a random, systematic, or dollar unit basis related to some quantity in the record.

Stratify. Stratify records based on quantities, or age records based on dates.

Calculations. Set up equations to perform calculations using quantities within records and constants outside of records.

Sequence records. Use quantities, dates, or names to sort records in alpha or numeric sequence in an ascending or descending order. This process can be used to identify gaps and duplications in a sequence.

Summarize. Count records, and total, subtotal, or classify quantities within records.

Create files and records. Produce new files and records. Merge or append files. Compare files, and add new fields and data to records.

Documentation. The processes performed on imported files are automatically documented.

Exportation. Export processed files in a wide variety of formats for additional processing in other software packages.

Here are two example applications:

Customer Credit Limit Analysis

Sampling revealed that customer credit limits were not always being followed. To determine the full extent of this problem, an analysis was performed. The client's customer master file contained credit limits. The credit limit for each customer was compared to the receivables master file. A report was produced showing each customer that had exceeded his or her credit limit and the amount of that excess credit. Excess credit did, indeed, account for an unacceptable percentage of total receivables.

Inventory Turnover Analysis

Rising inventory investment suggested obsolescence or slow movement for inventory items held by a small manufacturer. An inventory turnover analysis would clarify this problem. Withdrawals from inventory by item were stratified by age. The client's master inventory permanent records file for each of the last three years were appended to make up one file. Ranges of 180 days each were set up to cover the three-year period. A stratification report was produced showing the number of withdrawals for each range for each inventory item and the current percentage value of each item of total current inventory value. The report revealed that, for a number of items, there were rapidly declining withdrawals over the six ranges with a resulting increase in proportionate inventory value for those items.

WORD PROCESSING

The only efficient and effective way to prepare advisory comments, management letters, and reports is to use a word processor. The advantages are overwhelming. Most of the popular word-processing packages such as Microsoft Word and WordPerfect offer similar basic advantages.

You can achieve tremendous savings in time and effort through the ease of:

- Correcting, editing, and formatting documents.
- Copying, storing, and retrieving documents.
- Printing documents.

Here is a brief review of features that further enhance the value of word processing:

Typefaces and sizes. Select from a variety of typefaces (fonts) and sizes to prepare a document with a professional finish. Italics, boldface, and other type styling capabilities increase the interest of the reader. They also allow you to place emphasis where you want it. Here is a part of an advisory comment as printed on the typewriter:

```
Benefits of selling obsolete inventory


    The inventory analysis identified 32 obsolete com-
ponents making up 7 percent of total inventory value.
These are the benefits of selling these components:

  • Tax write-off. The difference between actual
    cost and the lower sales price for this inventory
    can be claimed as a loss for tax purposes. The
    effect is lower taxes.

  • Increased revenue. Funds invested in this
    inventory are unproductive for the company. Cash
    received from its sale would improve the
    company's cash flow.

  • Cut losses. This inventory continues to decline
    in value and continues to occupy costly storage
    space. By selling this inventory now, the company
    would minimize these losses.
```

Here is the same advisory comment printed through a word processor:

BENEFITS OF SELLING OBSOLETE INVENTORY

The inventory analysis identified 32 obsolete components making up 7 percent of total inventory value. These are the benefits of selling these components:

- **Tax write-off.** The difference between actual cost and the lower sales price for this inventory can be claimed as a loss for tax purposes. The effect is *lower taxes.*
- **Increased revenue.** Funds invested in this inventory are unproductive for the company. Cash received from its sale would *improve the company's cash flow.*
- **Cut losses.** This inventory continues to decline in value and continues to occupy costly storage space. By selling this inventory now, the company would *minimize these losses.*

Which of these two formats sends the message most effectively?

     Templates. Use standard document templates (formats) or custom design templates, and store them for future use. Formatting features such as multiple columns, repeated page headings, or repeated page footings are stored in the template.

     Spelling checker. Spelling checkers automatically verify the spelling of words in your document by comparing those words to a stored dictionary. They also suggest alternative spellings. If you wish to retain your own more creative spellings, the spelling checker allows you to do so. Using the spelling checker spares you the embarrassment of misspellings in a document sent to the client.

     Grammar checker. Grammar checkers identify long sentences, the passive voice (see Chapter 7), and other writing problems. They report the number of words in the document and calculate its reading level (see Chapter 7). Grammar checkers perform all of these tasks automatically within a couple of minutes. The grammar checker helps you significantly improve the readability of your advisory comments.

     Import and export. The major word processors permit importation and conversion of files produced by other word-processing software. Many word processors also permit export or conversion of files to other word-processing software.

Scanning converts printed documents into computerized images. Character recognition programs then convert these images into word-processing files. The hardware and software for scanning are relatively inexpensive. The scanning process saves you the effort of retyping client documents if you wish to include them with advisory comments.

In view of these advantages, there is no reasonable alternative to computerized word processing. Many word-processing packages also include basic graph capabilities.

GRAPHS

We are visually oriented. If the image is right for the purpose, it telegraphs the message much more quickly than words. For both financial and nonfinancial viewers, graphs demonstrate trends, relationships, and proportions much better than tables. This ease of communication makes the graph a powerful tool for persuasion. There are other good reasons for using graphs:

Graphs distill the message. A well-designed graph presents relationships with great clarity. It is the essence of the message uncluttered by context. Large volumes of information are compressed and summarized in graphs. This feature of graphs makes them very useful in decision making.

Graphs repeat the message. To reinforce a message, present it in different modes. Graphs remain interesting even though they repeat a written message.

Graphs create a positive impression. The presence of graphs in advisory comments suggest the writer invested care and thought in preparing the advisory comments.

Graphs dramatize the message. Because of the space they occupy, graphs distinguish the message and assert its importance.

For all of these reasons, graphs should be used much more frequently in advisory comments.

Graph Software Features

Very sophisticated graph packages are available. These provide such features as regression smoothing of line graphs, logarithmic scaling, or images of extremely high resolution. For most purposes, the graphing function of popular word processors is adequate and even impressive. Any graphing software should include the following features, whether the software is integral to a word processor or is an independent graph program:

- A variety of graph types including column, bar, pie, area, and line graphs.
- Scaling and sizing functions that permit manual revision.
- Label, caption, and legend features allowing the use of different typefaces and sizes.
- Editing and relocating capacity for labels, captions, and legends.
- Editing capability for the graph as a whole so that it can be revised without reconstruction.
- A wide variety of line and patterning options.
- Capacity to accept imported data sets for graphing.
- Comprehensive and clearly written reference or instruction manuals.

Types of Graphs

We'll review the uses and software design features for pie graphs, column graphs, area graphs, and line graphs.

Pie graphs.   Pie graphs are useful for showing proportionate shares of a whole. They are not helpful in presenting qualitatively different or disparate factors. The number of pie segments should be limited to five or six. Otherwise the graph becomes cluttered and too difficult to interpret. Note in Figure 6–1 how the significant segment (Customer A/R in excess of credit limits) is

FIGURE 6-1
Pie Graph

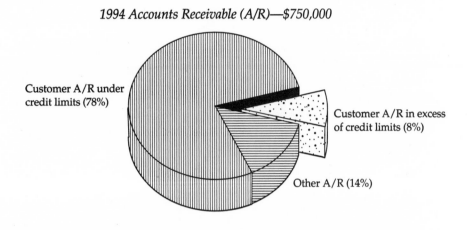

1994 Accounts Receivable (A/R)—$750,000

Customer A/R under credit limits (78%)

Customer A/R in excess of credit limits (8%)

Other A/R (14%)

emphasized by pulling it out of the pie. Choose contrasting patterning for segments to avoid confusion of segments. Labels should be on or close to the segments they identify.

Design options for pie graphs include:

- Representing the pie in two or three dimensions.
- Displacing segments.
- Labeling segments by means of arrows or a key to the segment patterns.
- Tilting the plane of the pie in relation to the viewer.
- Rotating the pie to position important segments.
- Selecting from a wide variety of patterns for segments or background.

Column graphs. Column graphs are probably the most easily understood of graph types. They can show relationships of different factors for a single time period or changes over several time periods to reveal trends. Note that each bar in the graph in Figure 6–2 shows relative quantities of product sales as well as total

FIGURE 6–2
Column Graph

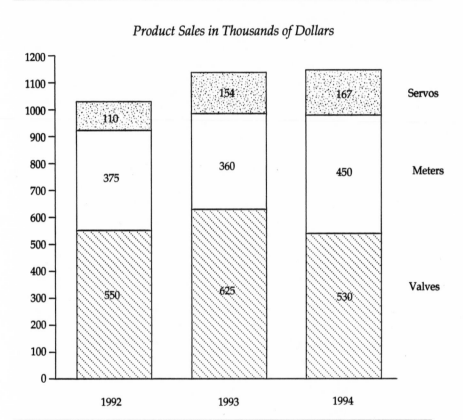

Product Sales in Thousands of Dollars

sales. Scaling can lead to misinterpretation of data presented in column graphs. In designing column graphs, one should try to ensure that the visual impression due to relative column height fairly represents changes in quantities. Adjacent columns or adjacent column segments should contain contrasting patterning.

Design options for column graphs include:

- Varying the width and spacing of columns.
- Representing columns in two or three dimensions.

- Presenting data on three scales for true three-dimensional scaling.
- Selecting from a wide variety of patterns for columns.
- Including or excluding grid lines.

Bar graphs. Bar graphs are similar to column graphs, only there is a horizontal orientation.

FIGURE 6–3
Area Graph

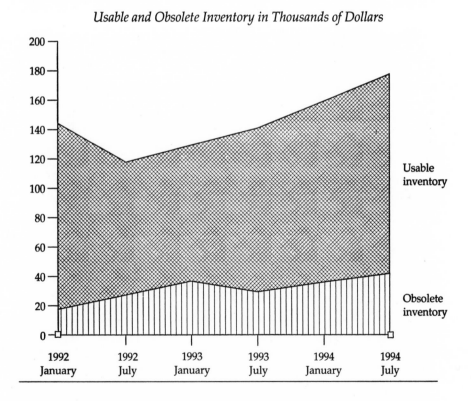

Usable and Obsolete Inventory in Thousands of Dollars

Area graphs. Area graphs are similar to line graphs except that they show an additive relationship of the different quantities graphed. They are often used to present changes over time. The area graph in Figure 6–3 shows obsolete inventory as a subtotal of total inventory (usable and obsolete inventory).

Design options for area graphs include:

- Representing area in two or three dimensions.
- Presenting several areas on three scales for true three-dimensional scaling.
- Selecting from a wide variety of patterns for areas.
- Including or excluding grid lines.

FIGURE 6–4
Line Graph

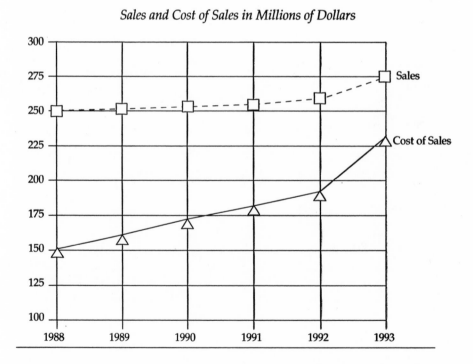

Sales and Cost of Sales in Millions of Dollars

Line graphs. Line graphs relate trends of either similar or different factors. They can be used to plot projections, showing both historical and projected trends. The line graph in Figure 6–4 clearly shows a trend of diminishing margin between sales and cost of sales.

Try to limit line graphs to no more that three lines. Use multiple graphs to show additional trends. Where marked changes on a line graph relate to some specific event, an arrow and label can call attention to the event.

Design options for line graphs include:

- Presenting lines in two or three dimensions.
- Marking lines with symbols to improve clarity.
- Using logarithmic scaling.
- Showing ranges of values by using vertical lines.
- Including or excluding grid lines.

IN SUMMARY

Microcomputers are especially valuable in preparing advisory comments. They help us uncover problems by enabling us to examine client databases. They help us present our comments in a persuasive manner through word processors and graphing software. A small accounting or consulting firm that fully exploits microcomputer capabilities can prepare far more useful and persuasive advisory comments than major firms that neglect this valuable tool.

Chapter Seven

Writing Guidelines

OVERVIEW

If you wish to write persuasive business advisory comments, then you must write them so they are easily understood. This chapter shows you how to apply guidelines to make your writing more readable. It also explains how to avoid common faults that confuse or obscure your message to the client.

THE GUIDELINES

There are guidelines for readable writing. They apply to business advisory comments. Readable writing is clear, simple, and direct. These are the guidelines:

- Use short words.
- Use short sentences.
- Write concisely.
- Use active verbs.
- Choose words carefully.

Why is it important to follow these guidelines in writing advisory comments?

- Your clients want information as easily as they can get it. These guidelines make the difference between "hard" reading and "easy" reading. That difference matters. If your advisory comments are easy to read, your client will *want* to read them.

- A valuable suggestion loses credibility if it's presented poorly. Clear, simple, and direct writing helps the client see the true merit of your suggestions.

- Aside from the opinion letter, the management letter is likely to be the only significant written report you regularly send to your client. So your client probably views the management letter as an indicator of the quality of your work. Pompous, confused, or obscure writing sends the wrong message.

Let's see how these guidelines can help your writing send the right message.

USE SHORT WORDS

As an auditor, you have two vocabularies. One of them is your vocabulary of technical terms. These terms are effective and efficient when you write for someone who shares your technical sophistication. When you are writing for peers or knowledgeable clients, they expect you to use your technical vocabulary. Often its use is virtually mandatory. So we'll call it your mandatory vocabulary.

You have another vocabulary that is nontechnical. It consists of all the words you use between technical terms. It also includes the words you use when you explain technical matters to someone who does *not* share your technical understanding. We'll call this your elective vocabulary. It's elective because, within it, you have a choice. You can choose between:

Facilitate or help

Magnitude or size

Demonstrate or show

Terminate or end

Anticipate or expect

Remunerate or pay

Endeavor or try

You have a choice between a long word or a short word that means the same thing. Where this choice exists, within your *elective* vocabulary, choose the short word. This is a guideline for your elective vocabulary and *not* for your mandatory vocabulary. Don't substitute short words for technical terms where technical terms would be more efficient.

This guideline raises two questions:

1. When should you use your mandatory (technical) vocabulary?

   Use technical terms when you know the client will understand them. Otherwise, explain the technical terms as you introduce them, or use other words in place of technical terms.

2. When should you use short words?

   Use short words when you are using your elective (nontechnical) vocabulary.

Let's see how this guideline applies to advisory comments:

We recommend that management implement procedures to guarantee accounts-receivable collections are monitored attentively and collection difficulties are resolved expeditiously.

Now we'll try to save on syllables without losing meaning:

We suggest that management take steps to ensure accounts-receivable collections are monitored closely and collection problems are solved quickly.

The words are shorter, and the comment is easier to read. Complicated concepts do not require long words. There's a special challenge in making a difficult idea easy to understand. Short words are precisely the tools you need to meet this challenge.

USE SHORT SENTENCES

At one time or another, you have come across sentences that were so long that you forgot the subject by the time you reached the end of the sentence and had to return to the beginning of the sentence to figure out what the writer wanted to say (a sentence like this one). Long sentences are annoying. They're an unnecessary burden for the reader.

For accountants and auditors, one motive for these run-on sentences is caution. Accountants and auditors tend to build up sentences according to this pattern:

- Subject.
- Subject + description.
- Subject + description + explanation.
- Subject + description + explanation + qualification.

Auditors may even tack on a disclaimer of all preceding clauses.

These sentences often exceed the number of clauses that can properly be crammed within grammatical boundaries. They are not run-on sentences, but marathon sentences. You can use two scalpels to cut run-on sentences into smaller ones.

1. Restate the subject.
2. Break the sentence where there's a change of idea.

Restate the subject. There's an alternative to "subject + description + explanation + qualification." It is:

- Subject + description.
- Subject + explanation.
- Subject + qualification.

There's nothing wrong with repeating the subject to cut your sentence length. Here's an example in need of radical surgery:

> For Henderson Savings and Loan, the allowable deduction under the percentage-of-taxable-income method is calculated by multiplying the association's taxable income (before bad-debt deduction and without net gains from the sale of corporate stock or municipal securities, and without certain dividends) by 8 percent and subtracting the current year's addition to the reserve for nonqualifying loans.

We'll break this sentence into shorter ones by restating the subject:

For Henderson Savings and Loan, the allowable deduction can be calculated under the percentage-of-taxable-income method. The allowable deduction is 8 percent of the association's taxable income less the current year's addition to the reserve for nonqualifying loans. The taxable income is before bad-debt deduction and without net gains from the sale of corporate stock or municipal securities, and without certain dividends.

Now you can get to the end of the sentence with the subject still in mind. You can use a pronoun in place of the subject when you're sure the object of the pronoun is clear to the reader.

Break the sentence at a change of idea. In a run-on sentence, there are usually several changes of idea. The changes may be signaled by conjunctions and prepositions. These are words such as: and, or, but, if, however, when, although, while, as, to, before, after. Consider this example:

Usually, the advantages of a buy–sell agreement or stock purchase agreement is that the stock of the corporation will not go to outsiders against the desire of other stockholders and to assure that, on the death of a stockholder, his or her investment in the corporation will be easily convertible to cash.

We'll break this sentence where there are changes in idea:

Usually, an advantage of a buy–sell agreement is that the stock of the corporation will not go to outsiders. Otherwise, persons could buy stock against the desires of other stockholders. The agreement also assures that, on the death of a stockholder, his or her investment in the corporation will be easily convertible to cash.

The average sentence length for business writing is 27 words. For professional writers, the average sentence length is 17 words. In your own writing, try to limit sentences to 20 words. There's a plus to short sentences. An occasional short sentence adds "punch" and variety to your writing. Periods are free. Use a lot of them.

WRITE CONCISELY

One of the differences between spoken language and written language is in the use of filler words. When speaking, we use filler words to provide thought continuity in time. We use filler words to gain time to think and to signal listeners that we have more to say on the subject. In writing, continuity is provided by the printed words, sentences, and paragraphs on the page. Filler words aren't needed. Yet because of this habit of speech, we use filler words in our writing. Our writing becomes inflated when we use filler words, wordy phrases, and redundancies.

Here's an example of a wordy business advisory comment:

> To further enhance the Company's overall cash management, we recommend that the Company reconsider its current policies governing cash payments. The Company has failed to take full advantage of cash discounts provided by some vendors. In addition, it may be appropriate to consider negotiating set prices from certain primary suppliers in exchange for a commitment from the Company to purchase material from those primary suppliers.

There are 65 words in this comment. Our goal is to cut unnecessary words. By doing so, we can state virtually the same message in only 34 words:

> To improve cash management, the Company should change its payment procedures to take advantage of vendor cash discounts. Also, the Company should try to secure discounts from primary suppliers in exchange for purchase commitments.

The message is more direct, and the meaning is clearer. We have written economically but not telegraphically.

Wordy phrases are a common cause of inflated writing. Check your advisory comments for any of these wordy phrases and substitute a single word:

Wordy Phrase	**Alternative**
Inasmuch as	Since
With the exception of	Except
In order to	To
For the purpose of	To
In the neighborhood of	About
At the present time	Now
Make an examination of	Examine
During the course of	While

In the amount of	For
Due to the fact that	Because
In the event that	If
In the very near future	Soon

At the close of a letter, Mark Twain wrote, "I would have written a shorter letter, but I didn't have enough time." Winston Churchill said, "The time I spend writing a speech is inversely proportional to its length." Both writers are suggesting that concise writing takes time and effort. If you value your client, spending the time and effort is worthwhile.

USE ACTIVE VERBS

Verbs do the work in writing. Active verbs lift the ideas off the page and into the mind of the reader. We use active verbs when we write in the active voice. What's the difference between the active voice and the passive voice?

• In the active voice, the subject of the sentence performs the action:

The auditor observed the physical inventory.

The subject (auditor) performed the action (observed the physical inventory).

• In the passive voice, the subject of the sentence is acted upon:

The physical inventory was observed by the auditor.

The subject (physical inventory) was acted upon (observed by the auditor).

The passive voice requires more words than the active voice to say the same thing. The passive voice is used much more often in writing than in speech. It sounds a little unnatural in comparison to typical spoken language. "I reviewed the schedule of fixed assets." That's active. "The schedule of fixed assets was reviewed by me." That's passive. If we only wrote as we spoke, we wouldn't be troubled with the passive voice.

In the passive voice, the performer of the action may be omitted altogether:

The decision was made to shut down the Poughkeepsie plant.

We don't know who made the decision. Some people use the passive voice to avoid responsibility. The passive voice is bureaucratic and impersonal.

Here's an advisory comment in the *passive voice:*

The continued growth of the Company requires that management adopt procedures for the budgeting of operations and the forecasting of cash requirements. More efficient use of capital, the comparison of operating results with goals, and more effective decision making can be achieved by management through these procedures.

We can improve this comment a lot by using the *active voice* to put the cart *after* the horse.

Due to the Company's continued growth, management should adopt procedures to budget operations and forecast cash requirements. These procedures help management use capital more efficiently, compare operating results to goals, and make decisions more effectively.

Active verbs increase the interest and vitality of your writing. There's a measure of this vitality called the power/load ratio. It's based on the concept that, in any sentence, active verbs are the power and all the other words are the load. The ratio is the average number of active verbs to the average number of other words in the sentence:

$$\text{Power/load ratio} = \frac{\text{Average number of active verbs in sentence}}{\text{Average number of other words in sentence}}$$

For spoken language, the usual power/load ratio is one active verb for eight other words. In writing by professional authors, the power/load ratio is 1:10. Typically, in writing by business people, it's 1:25. That makes most business writing pretty dull. Since it has a conservative and impersonal tone, the passive voice is tempting to use in advisory comments. But your advisory comments will be more interesting (and more likely to be read) if they're in the active voice.

If you use a word processor, you can buy software that reviews word processing files (*Right Writer, Grammatik*). Some word processors include a grammar function (see Chapter 6). The software flags the passive voice. Most of us are unaware that our writing is passive. By calling your attention to the passive voice, this software feature gives you the option of changing passive writing to active writing. Usually, that change is a big improvement. The same software also flags run-on sentences and measures readability automatically.

MEASURING READABILITY

At this point, you understand the basic guidelines for readability. These are short words, short sentences, concise writing, and the active voice. These guidelines are used in measuring readability. Most systems for measuring readability assign a reading level according to public school grade. For example, the *Wall Street Journal* has an 11th grade readability level. The *Harvard Business Review* has a 17th grade readability level. This chapter has an 8th grade readability level.

If you use a word processor, the modest cost of review software such as *Right Writer* or *Grammatik* is worthwhile. The software is easy to use. It helps you improve readability by computing your readability index automatically. Try to write with a readability index of 12 or lower. Why should you write at a 12th grade level when your clients are college educated?

Research has shown again and again that readers prefer to read at a level below their capacity. You prefer to read below your capacity, just as you prefer to use the elevator even though you *can* walk up to the tenth floor. As a reader, you want information as easily as you can get it. So does your client. Neither you nor your client wants to struggle with long sentences and big words if you can avoid it. So it's a good idea to check the readability index of your advisory comments.

CHOOSE WORDS CAREFULLY

There are three criteria you can use to guide word choice. Here they are in their order of importance:

1. Clarity.
2. Brevity.
3. Elegance.

If you concentrate on applying the first two, there's very little scope for elegance. And that's the way it should be. Elegance is a distant third because our clients want functional writing and not artistic writing. Some word usage problems occur often in advisory comments. In pursuit of clarity and brevity, we'll discuss the solutions for these problems:

- Abstract or general words.
- Gobbledygook.
- Technobabble.
- Overcautious writing.
- Apologetic phrases.
- We-centered writing.

Abstract words or general words. Words stand for meanings. Those meanings are not in the words themselves. They are in the minds of the readers. Since no two minds are exactly alike, words are understood more or less differently depending on the experience of the reader.

This ambiguity in the meaning of words can frustrate communications. The problem is compounded by general or abstract words. General or abstract words have more meanings than concrete and specific words. When we use general words where we could use specific words, we add to the burden of the reader in trying to grasp our meaning. When we use general words unnecessarily, we ask the reader to sift through all the possible meanings to find the one we intend. That's work for the reader. To reduce that work, we should use words with the narrowest meaning, considering the context. In short, be specific.

There are catchall words that are convenient for the writer, but confusing for the reader. They're used in this example:

Because of several factors, the Company failed to meet certain conditions which resulted in the present situation.

What were the factors? What were the conditions? What is the situation? Here the reader needs some specific help.

Because the Company lost a major customer and raw materials cost increased, the Company defaulted on a loan. This default resulted in its low credit rating.

If you use the following words in an advisory comment, think again. Maybe you can be more specific.

Circumstances.

Conditions.

Considerations.

Elements.

Factors.

Influences.

Items.

Situations.

Gobbledygook. This word derives from the cry of the turkey. It describes useless or meaningless expressions in writing. Gobbledygook is seen a lot in government publications. There's gobbledygook outside government and outside the barnyard. We see it in business writing and in management advisory comments. In this example, the flow of ideas is clogged by gobbledygook:

We understand that the extent of segregation of duties is limited in terms of the number of personnel available. Due to the fact there were recent staff reductions, we are of the opinion that duty assignments should be reconsidered.

Many of these expressions serve no purpose. Even worse, they give the comment a pompous tone. Let's cut the gobbledygook:

The number of available personnel can limit segregation of duties. We believe duty assignments should be reconsidered due to recent staff reductions.

Here's a list of gobbledygook and recommended alternatives:

Gobbledygook	Alternative
Needless to say	(If it's needless, don't say it)
Which should be self-explanatory	(Insulting—delete)
At your earliest convenience	Soon (or a specific date)
In terms of	(Usually meaningless, delete)
As you know	(Delete)
Meet with approval	Be approved
It should be noted that	(Delete)
Pursuant to your request	As you requested
We are of the opinion	We believe
Please do not hesitate to	Please (or delete)
Please be advised	(Delete)
Please find enclosed	Enclosed is

Technobabble. Some auditors believe that technical terms should be used to impress the client, even where those terms are unnecessary. Here's an example:

Using standard software, the cost savings model was evaluated four times (iterations), with each iteration producing refinement in the data, the model, or both. After the fourth iteration, there was no significant improvement in the data.

"Iteration" is "computerese" for a repeated program. But the writer is describing *evaluation*. Why use unnecessary technical terms? These sentences in plain English are easier to understand:

Using standard software, the cost savings model was evaluated four times, with each evaluation producing a refinement in the data, the model, or both. After the fourth evaluation, there was no significant improvement in the data.

Technical terminology should make communication more efficient. Used otherwise, technical terms are technobabble.

Overcautious writing. Qualification is often necessary, but a fact remains a fact and should not be qualified. When you state your observations (rather than your opinions), avoid these phrases:

It appears that
One might infer
It would seem to be that
It may be appropriate to consider

Excessive hedging in an advisory comment weakens the auditor's credibility. Here's an example with the hedging italicized:

Based on our discussions with employees, *it appears that* the Company has a problem regarding employee morale. Employees *seem* to lack interest in their jobs and *we suspect* they lack pride in the Company.

Is there a morale problem, or not? Do employees lack interest and pride, or do they not? If the auditor can't answer these questions definitely, what's the value of his or her discussion with employees? This comment is so tentative the client can reasonably wonder why the auditor wrote it.

Apologetic phrases. Advisory comments sometimes include phrases that are too deferential. Here are some examples:

Permit us to say
We hope we can say that
With your indulgence
Please rest assured that

These and similar phrases don't accord with the auditor's independent and professional stature.

We-centered writing. You were introduced to the problem of "we-centered" writing in Chapter 4, *Advisory Comments: The Political Context*. There are two aspects to this problem. First, "we-centered writing" puts the auditor in the spotlight when the client should be in the spotlight. Second, using the pronoun "we" repeatedly can be boring and confusing for the reader. At some point, the reader may wonder who "we" refers to. Does "we" mean the:

- Writer?
- Firm?
- Auditor?
- Auditor *and* the reader?

Here's an advisory comment dominated by "we":

> *We* understand your concern about increasing audit fees. *We* believe that fees could be lowered if your bookkeeping staff could devote more of their time to the audit. *We* suggest that your bookkeeping staff could prepare a number of schedules that *we* have prepared in the past. It would be helpful if *we* could meet to discuss your staff's capabilities in preparing schedules required for the audit. *We* hope that *we* could develop a timetable for preparing schedules that would not burden your staff during periods of peak demand.

"We" is used seven times. Now let's put the emphasis where it belongs:

> Your concern about rising audit fees is very reasonable. If your bookkeeping staff could devote more time to the audit, fees could be lowered. Your bookkeeping staff could prepare many of the schedules that are presently prepared by us. Let's meet to discuss your staff's ability to prepare these schedules. Together, *we* could develop a time table for preparing the schedules so the work would not burden your staff during periods of peak demand.

"We" is used only once and in a way that suggests a benefit for the client. The client, not the auditor, is in the spotlight.

SMOOTHING THE PATH FOR YOUR CLIENT

Here are some additional suggestions for the format and content of the management letter and business advisory comments. By following them, you'll remove some pitfalls and roadblocks from the path of the client as he or she reads your writing.

Check grammar, spelling, punctuation, and word usage. There's an aura effect when your advisory comments contain errors in grammar, spelling, punctuation, and word usage. If the client recognizes such errors, he or she is likely to doubt the accuracy of facts or the validity of reasoning in the advisory comments. If you're not sure, check. Use the dictionary. Also, use the spell-checker of your word processor.

Spell out abbreviations. Spell out abbreviations and acronyms the first time you use them. Here's an example:

Just-In-Time (JIT) inventory methods lower inventory costs.

Don't make your client ask for the meanings of CAD (Computer-Aided Design), CAM (Computer-Aided Manufacturing), and CIM (Computer-Integrated Manufacturing). There was a time when you didn't know what they meant.

Meaningful statistics. Some statistics stand alone. Example: "Profit was 12.7 percent." Other statistics are basically comparative. Example: "Inventory turnover was 2.7." This ratio is not truly helpful unless it's related to an industry average or a trend. Provide comparative data where it's helpful. Explain or interpret statistics for your client, and show their relevance or importance. Shorten quantities to their useful significance. It makes them easier to understand. At the same time, you will avoid false precision.

Break up the page. Large blocks of copy intimidate readers. They don't want to begin reading if they can't see breaks in the copy. Break up the page using these techniques:

- Headings and subheadings.
- Paragraphing.
- Bullets.
- Numerical listing.
- White space.

Headings and subheadings. In Chapter 4, *Advisory Comments: The Political Context*, we suggested using headings that emphasize the benefit of the advisory comment. When a single advisory comment is very long, subheadings should be used within the comment. You might use subheadings that specifically describe the symptom, problem, solution, and benefit. For example, a long advisory comment on accounts receivable management might have these headings:

Improving cash flow

Number of days sales in receivables

Large receivables investment

Suggested collection procedures

Lowered receivables investment

Note the benefits heading and how the subheadings follow the pattern of symptom, problem, solution, and benefit. They almost tell the story.

Paragraphing.   Paragraph frequently. Skipping a line, or skipping a line and indenting, is better than indenting alone. Skipping a line clearly breaks up the copy into digestible pieces. Try not to exceed 12 lines for each paragraph.

Bullets.   Use bullets for a short list of items when there is no specific sequence or order of importance in the listing. Bullets are helpful in introductions and summaries.

Numerical listing.   To emphasize sequence, order of inclusion, or order of importance, number the items. If there is a long list and you will refer to specific items in the list, numerical references are helpful.

White space.   Although you want to break up the page, you don't want a cluttered appearance. White space helps prevent clutter. Indent tables, columns, and long quotations. Use generous margins. It's better to use too much white space than too little. There's a bonus to white space. It adds importance to the content.

GRAPHS

As an auditor, you easily grasp the significance of financial quantities. Not so for many clients. Line graphs, pie charts, and column charts help them visualize problems, solutions, trends, and projections that may be obvious to you from the raw data. Follow these suggestions for more understandable graphs:

- For line graphs, try to avoid more than three lines on the same graph. Multiple graphs will be clearer than many lines on the same graph.
- Use pie charts to show parts in relation to the whole. Limit pie charts to five segments. If you have more than five segments, consider using a bar chart.
- If several graphs are related, use the same scale for easier comparison.
- Don't group graphs in a separate section. Insert them in the copy where they are discussed.
- Make sure labeling and titles are complete and clear.
- Events, important quantities, and key points can be called out by using arrows on the graph.
- Explain key points of the graph in the text.

Graphs are discussed further in Chapter 6, *Help from the Microcomputer*.

PROOFREADING

Use the same care in proofreading the advisory comments that you use in proofreading the opinion letter and financial statements. Several readings will be needed.

On the first reading, check for:

- Sense.
- Accuracy.
- Completeness.
- Readability.
- Consistency.

On the second reading, check for:

- Grammar.
- Spelling.
- Punctuation.
- Word usage.

On the third reading, check for the correctness of:

- Names and titles.
- Headings and subheadings.
- Labels, captions, and exhibits.
- All internal cross references.

Appendix B contains a *Business Advisory Comment Checklist* that should help you catch errors.

IN SUMMARY

There are some overall goals you expect to achieve through your writing in business advisory comments:

- To inform.
- To document.
- To persuade

If your goal is to inform, then the writing guidelines we've discussed help you reach your goal by cutting the "noise" of confusing and unnecessary words so your message gets through. The guidelines simplify the conversion of printed symbols into ideas or mental images.

If your goal is to document a problem, the guidelines help you avoid misinterpretations that could create difficulties in the future. There may be legal liability exposure in ambiguous or confused writing. By following the guidelines, you help minimize that exposure.

If your goal is to persuade, then the guidelines help by ensuring your writing will be understood. "Easy" reading is surely more persuasive than "hard" reading.

If impressing the client with your command of the language is the goal, the question in your mind is: "What will the reader thing of me?" Ego-involved, wordy, and pompous writing is the result.

If impressing the client with your ability to solve the client's problems is the goal, the question in your mind is: "Will the reader understand this?" Clear, simple, and direct writing is the result.

We are not poets. The message is lost the moment our writing calls attention to itself. For our purposes, writing should be transparent. It's the content that counts.

Chapter Eight

Example Advisory Comments

OVERVIEW

These example advisory comments refer to different clients. They are not excerpted from a single management letter. They illustrate a wide variety of problems and concerns. They also show how the guidelines for writing advisory comments are applied.

Example advisory comments deal with these issues:

Capital expenditure budgeting
Budgeting
Discounts for timely payments
Fixed-asset record keeping
Inventory—cycle counting
Just-in-time (JIT) inventory management
Microcomputer purchasing
Physical inventory
Receivables management
Strategic planning
Tax deduction
Vendor overcharges

GREATER BENEFIT FROM CAPITAL EXPENDITURES

In 1990, Shoe Tree spent $85,000 to upgrade wood shaping equipment. Shortly after this equipment purchase, Shoe Tree decided to convert to plastic injection molding for its main line of shoe trees. Lowered costs, improved designs, and increased sales amply justified the conversion. But the expenditure for wood shapers proved unnecessary. That expenditure is symptomatic of the need for capital expenditure budgets. Fixed asset additions increased by about 15 percent per year over the last three years. Shoe Tree can reduce the disproportionate increase through capital expenditure budgeting.

Shoe Tree has a long-range goal of plant relocation in five years. Shoe Tree cannot realistically achieve this goal without current capital expenditure budgeting. Some members of management believe their capital expenditure requests deserve more consideration. These views suggest that better communication would help in determining capital expenditures.

Capital expenditure budgeting involves a semiannual review of needs and available resources. A capital budget committee evaluates and sets priorities for all proposed capital expenditures. The committee might consist of President Joe Welch, Financial Vice-President Ron Kay, Marketing Vice-President Mary Sims, and Plant Manager Arnold Doyle. The committee would consider proposed expenditures in relation to plans, available resources, extent of the need, and the probable cost/benefit ratio for Shoe Tree. The committee would also recommend specific capital sources and the timing of expenditures.

Capital expenditure budgeting places additional demands on the time and attention of management. The payoff for increased management concern is well worth the effort. The capital expenditure budgeting process offers these very important advantages for Shoe Tree:

- Greater value received for each dollar of capital expenditure.

- Lowered cost of capital through more effective use of Shoe Tree's resources.

- Improved timing of expenditures to exploit temporary financial opportunities.

- More effective decisions as to the nature of capital expenditures.

- Better support for Shoe Tree's short- and long-range plans.

- Improved communication, understanding, and commitment by members of the management team concerning capital expenditures.

Next November, the board of Directors will decide whether to decrease retained earnings for the previous year. By implementing capital budgeting now, management could provide budgeted capital expenditures as useful and timely input for the board's decision in November.

PROFIT IMPROVEMENT THROUGH BUDGETING

During Gastronaut's early years of growth, limited cash flow was a natural check on spending. Now cash flow problems have eased and Gastronaut Foods' position has large profit potential. But Gastronaut may not realize those profits. Last year, cost of operations as a percentage of net sales rose from 72 percent to 83 percent. This is 8 percent higher than the average for its industry and sales volume. Profits will continue to decline unless Gastronaut controls operating costs.

Budgeting effectively controls costs and it has additional advantages. As an initial step, bookkeeping could prepare a quarterly report of the 20 largest operating accounts each for purchasing, canning, warehousing, and shipping and receiving. A quarterly report is helpful since cost overruns usually occur during peak canning periods. This report becomes a basis for cost studies and recommendations within each department. The accounts are budget-line items subject to future refinement. Last year's average amounts for each account could serve as initial targets for this year. Each operating department head analyzes important departures from targeted amounts and explains those departures to the executive committee.

These measures are only the first step in developing a budget system. Eventually, a budget system should evolve through incremental improvements, tailored to the specific needs of Gastronaut Foods. This budget system could rely, in part, on marketing forecasts. Marketing lags canning by about three to four months. So

controlling canning costs of seasonal harvests in relation to marketing forecasts is a difficult assignment. But the effort should be
well rewarded. Gastronaut should receive these advantages from
a budget system:

- Help in spotting exceptional cost trends so they can be
  quickly corrected.
- An increased management sense of accountability for costs.
- Analytical reviews of factors contributing to costs.
- Meaningful goals for financial performance and cost control.
- Improved financial and operations planning.
- Measurable progress in cost reduction.

If Gastronaut effectively implements budgetary steps this year
and other conditions are the same, Gastronaut's pre-tax net profit
as a percentage of net sales could improve from 3.4 percent this
year to 4.4 percent next year.

LOWERED COSTS THROUGH
TIMELY PAYMENTS

A sample of 250 invoices included 38 offering timely payment
discounts of 5 percent to 15 percent. None of these discounts
were exploited. The total of the 38 invoices was $11,500. At 7.5
percent, discounts could have amounted to about $870. The com-
pany paid 3,750 invoices in 1993. Accordingly, overlooked discounts amounted to about $13,000.

A 5 percent discount does not sound like a lot, but it is the
approximate equivalent of a 60 percent annual interest rate.
Clearly, this is a much higher return than the company could
achieve from any internal or external investment.

The bookkeeping costs to benefit from these discounts are neg-
ligible. The bookkeeper should sort incoming invoices and sep-
arately batch those offering timely payment discounts. These invoices should receive priority treatment and be paid in time to
realize the discounts.

These are the benefits of exploiting timely payment discounts:

- Lowered costs totaling approximately $13,000.
- Improved cash flow.
- Improved relations with vendors.

IMPROVED EFFICIENCY FOR FIXED-ASSET RECORD KEEPING

Fixed-asset additions occur irregularly. As a result, it is easy to overlook necessary updates of fixed-asset records. Your fixed-asset records reflect this problem. Your 1993 acquisition of two milling machines and a punch press were not recorded. Depreciation was not regularly calculated nor correctly calculated. Fixed-asset records should include the following detail:

- Description.
- Depreciable life.
- Location.
- Depreciation method.
- Purchase date.
- Current year's depreciation expense.
- Cost.
- Accumulated depreciation.

Maintaining this detail need not be a significant burden to bookkeeping. You could minimize bookkeeping effort by purchasing inexpensive software that performs this function. This software costs between $700 and $900. The software is compatible with your present system. It has these helpful features:

- Prompts for recording required data.
- Automatically calculates current and accumulated depreciation.
- Automatically formats and produces schedules and reports.

Your company would benefit from acquiring this software in these ways:

- Current and accurate fixed-asset records for control purposes.
- Planning data for future fixed-asset acquisitions.
- Reduced bookkeeping time and effort.
- Appropriate records to support tax returns and insurance claims.

SAVINGS IN PHYSICAL-INVENTORY COSTS

Electroparts has developed an excellent computerized perpetual inventory record system. Due to the close supervision of Janet Strong, the system produces useful, timely, and reliable reports. For the last three years, there has been less that a .5 percent difference between inventory valuations based on physical inventory counts and perpetual records.

The annual physical inventory is a complete count of all trade inventory. This count requires one week's work of seven clerks under the supervision of the controller. The cost of this physical inventory amounts to about $6,500.

Because the difference between physical inventory and perpetual records has been so small, management may wish to reduce physical inventory costs through cycle counting. In cycle counting, high-value items are counted more often than other items. The results are used to verify the reliability of the perpetual inventory system. Your perpetual inventory system could produce an ABC inventory classification for use in designing cycle counts.

Cycle counting could reduce physical inventory costs by about 50 percent. Your saving could amount to about $3,250. We would be happy to advise you in designing a cycle counting program for your inventory.

SAVINGS IN INVENTORY INVESTMENT AND STORAGE COSTS

Comfy Furniture recently installed more versatile production machinery, freeing space on the plant floor formerly used by older, special-purpose machines. Management has considered this space as usable for potential plant expansion. For 1990, sales volume increased 3 percent. For 1991 through 1993, sales volume has remained virtually constant. In view of these market trends for Comfy's upholstered chairs, expansion of production capacity is unlikely.

Storing standard fabrics, springs, and framing lumber requires 70,000 square feet of leased warehouse space at $1.85 per square foot per year. This amounts to an annual leasing cost of $129,500.

Management is committed to a value-added perspective in reducing costs. From the customer viewpoint, storage of raw materials adds nothing to the value of the furniture. Management can achieve both reduced raw-materials storage cost and lower raw-materials investment by initiating a Just-In-Time (JIT) raw-materials inventory program. With some adjustment, recently freed space on the plant floor permits spotting raw materials close to the appropriate machinery.

A JIT raw-materials inventory program has these advantages for Comfy Furniture:

- Significantly reduced leased-storage-space cost.
- Productive use of idle plant floor space.
- Significantly reduced investment in raw-materials inventory.
- Reduced administrative and insurance costs for raw-materials inventory.

These advantages permit management to redirect resources from non-value-added activities to value-added activities.

Our staff includes a consultant highly experienced in developing JIT inventory and traffic-control programs for manufacturers of your sales volume. We would appreciate the opportunity of helping Comfy Furniture realize the significant benefits of a JIT inventory system. At your request, we would be happy to explore the feasibility of a JIT inventory program system and to submit a proposal for its development.

LOWER MICROCOMPUTER COSTS

Amy Wilson, reports manager, commented that word processing was sometimes slowed because document formatting produced different results on different microcomputers. Because of the different microcomputers, assistants had to rekey data occasionally. She also said that each of her assistants required training on different computers before they were sufficiently productive. She estimates that report production could increase by about 5 percent if these problems were solved. A surprising variety of microcomputers are in service at Weststar, Inc. These include:

Make	Number
Hewlett Packard	3
Compudyne	7
IBM	8
Macintosh	4

This variety of microcomputers results from independent purchasing decisions by members of management. Weststar's current investment in microcomputers is $67,300. Presently, management is considering purchasing six additional computers and installing a LAN. Six new computers and a LAN system will cost between $20,000 and $30,000. Members of management should study Weststar's microcomputer usage before adding to the present microcomputer investment. This study should identify the most cost-effective microcomputers to purchase considering the types of applications used by Weststar. The study should also seek to increase computer compatibility through any new purchases. Increased compatibility enables Weststar to maximize return on its existing microcomputer investment.

Because of their work with microcomputers, George Steed, office manager, and Amy Wilson, reports manager, are logical choices to conduct this study. Time and effort devoted to this study should have a large payoff in the benefits of increased computer compatibility. These benefits include:

- Increased efficiency in producing reports.

- Reduced training time for computer users.
- Lower costs for computer servicing contracts.
- Lower software costs.
- Simplified and more effective backup procedures.
- Improved virus protection.

Using Amy Wilson's estimate of a 5-percent improvement in report production applied to her department's payroll, the annual value of the benefit from her department alone would amount to about $9,000.

REDUCING BACK-ORDER RECEIVABLES

The following graph shows the gradually increasing average receivables collection period for Electroparts compared to the industry average.

Investigation shows that this increasing collection period is primarily due to increasing back-order receivables. These are partial shipments to customers that are not paid by customers until they receive completed shipments. The proportion of partial shipments to complete shipments has been increasing because of difficulties in sales forecasting and because of shipment delays by suppliers. For example, Wilcox Wire, your supplier of coaxial cables, has consistently shipped orders 30 to 45 days after the promised delivery date.

Management should evaluate a number of possible means of reducing back-order receivables. Here are some solutions that merit evaluation:

- Review receiving reports to identify suppliers with chronic shipping delays. Then locate alternative suppliers with equivalent prices and terms. For some items, it may not be possible to find alternative suppliers. Where feasible, change suppliers to assure on-time deliveries.
- Promptly inform customers that items they have ordered are back-ordered and that you will bill for partial shipments. Management must consider the way in which this practice might influence customer relations.

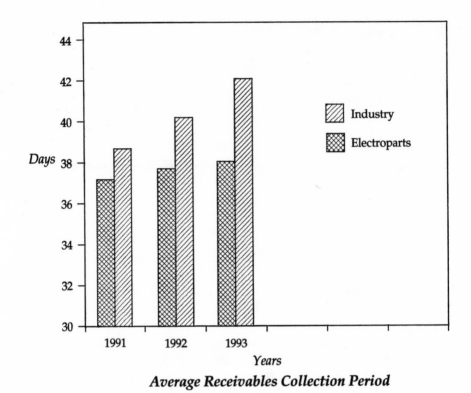

Average Receivables Collection Period

- Increase inventory levels of frequently back-ordered items to compensate for the suppliers' delivery delays. Of course, increased inventory investment is an additional cost.
- Conduct a study to improve the accuracy of sales forecasting.

Most of these solutions present disadvantages. After study, some combination of these steps might provide the best solution with minimum disadvantages.

Solving this problem has two important benefits for Electroparts. These are lowered receivables investment and greater customer satisfaction. Management could adopt the goal of the average industry collection period as a measure of its progress in solving this problem.

STRATEGIC PLANNING FOR
IMPROVED PROFITS

As a manufacturer of motorcycle parts, Rockford Company is in an industry under stress. Imports dominate 67.8 percent of the domestic market. The domestic market is shrinking, due in part, to an aging population and safety issues. Unit sales in the US market dropped 13 percent last year. There is over capacity in the industry and the pricing of foreign and domestic competitors is predatory. Rockford's losses of $250,000 in fiscal 1990 are understandable considering industry conditions.

Even in this hostile business environment, it is possible to improve Rockford's profit picture. For the industry, Rockford's cost of operations is relatively high. For a company with this sales volume, cost of operations as a percentage of net sales for the industry is 69.6 percent. The cost of operations as a percentage of net sales is 79 percent. Sales decreased by 15 percent last year, continuing a downward trend. These problems cannot successfully be tackled piecemeal. Solving these problems requires an overall approach. Consider these possible goals for restructuring manufacturing and marketing:

For manufacturing

- Reduce overhead and scrap losses.
- Acquire more versatile manufacturing equipment.
- Implement computer-aided manufacturing (CAM).

For marketing

- Focus on product differentiation rather than on direct price competition.
- Undertake market research for new product lines (product diversification).

Robert Casey, chief of production and Bill Kelsey, vice-president of marketing, suggested these possible goals. To some extent, the goals are interdependent. For example, product diversification is not feasible without more versatile manufacturing equipment. Achieving these or alternative goals requires overall planning. Rockford does not have a strategic business plan.

Strategic planning with realistic goals would help management direct efforts to specific areas that could provide leverage in improving profits. Participation in the planning process assures general understanding of the goals and helps secure management commitment and support. Strategic plans and goals would help management measure its progress and identify shortfalls for timely correction. If strategic planning were implemented and aggressively pursued, some profit improvement could be achieved by 1992.

ADDITIONAL TAX DEDUCTION

While reviewing Polymorphic's fixed asset depreciation schedules, we discovered an overlooked deduction. In 1993 Polymorphic Metals purchased a computer-operated production lathe. At the same time, it retired two turret lathes from service. No scrap payment was received for these lathes. The remaining undepreciated cost of these lathes is $4,250. This amount is deductible for 1993.

Annually, the chief accountant should review the schedule of fixed assets to identify any retired fixed assets with residual undepreciated costs. Such costs are deductible for the tax year in which the retirement occurs. This review will help assure that Polymorphic receives all the tax deductions to which it is entitled.

REDUCING VENDOR OVERCHARGES

A sampling of 250 purchase orders revealed three instances of vendor overcharges. These overcharges amounted to $653. To correct these overcharges, bookkeeping had to contact vendors. In some cases, delayed contact with vendors added to the vendors' difficulty in correcting the overcharges. Although these overcharges were corrected and refunded, bookkeeping may not have identified other overcharges. Your company issued 2,152 purchase orders last year. If the error rate is consistent, total over-charges would amount to about $2,500.

A very simple step would help to solve this problem. Purchase orders do not presently include the vendors' quoted price. Include the vendors' quoted price on the purchase order. When bookkeeping matches vendor invoices with purchase orders, the clerk can compare the quoted price and invoice charge. If the invoice charge exceeds the quoted price, the clerk would inform the appropriate manager so he or she can investigate and correct the error before bookkeeping pays the invoice.

By including the vendor's quoted price on the purchase order, Polymorphic would receive these advantages:

- Prompt correction of vendor invoice errors.
- Reduced vendor overcharges of about $2,500.
- Reduced bookkeeping effort in correcting overcharges.
- Improved vendor relations.

Appendix A

COMPREHENSIVE BUSINESS ADVISORY COMMENT SURVEY QUESTIONNAIRE

Contents

I. MANAGEMENT GOALS AND OBJECTIVES
  A. Management Goals and Objectives
  B. Entrepreneurial Goals and Objectives
  C. Short-Range, Long-Range, and Strategic Planning
  D. Budgeting
  E. Market Share and Industry Status
  F. Markets
  G. Territories and Siting
  H. Profitability
  I. Growth
  J. Continuity
  K. Performance Measures

II. CAPITAL AND FINANCIAL MANAGEMENT
  A. Equity
  B. Debt
  C. Fixed Assets
  D. Working Capital
  E. Cash Management
  F. Credit
  G. Receivables
  H. Billing
  I. Collections

   J.   Accounts Payable

III. ORGANIZATION
   A. Structure
   B. Organization
   C. Policy
   D. Authority and Responsibility
   E. Staffing
   F. Operating Procedures
   G. Office Procedures

IV. MARKETING
   A. Market Planning
   B. Customers
   C. Products and Product Planning
   D. Pricing
   E. Promotion and Advertising
   F. Retailing
   G. Sales Force
   H. Selling Costs
   I.   Order Processing
   J.   Servicing

V. PRODUCTION AND SERVICES
   A. Planning and Control
   B. Purchasing
   C. Supplier Relations
   D. Receiving
   E. Inventory Management
   F. Manufacturing
   G. Quality Control
   H. Supervision
   I.   Manufacturing and Labor Cost Control
   J.   Warehousing
   K. Shipping
   L. Facilities and Machinery

VI. HUMAN RESOURCES
  A. Workforce Planning and Utilization
  B. Personnel Administration
  C. Communications
  D. Recruiting and Hiring
  E. Training
  F. Safety
  G. Compensation and Benefits
  H. Evaluation
  I. Law and Regulations
  J. Unions

VII. MANAGEMENT INFORMATION AND CONTROLS
  A. General Ledger System
  B. Financial Statements
  C. Management Information Systems
  D. Electronic Data Processing

I. MANAGEMENT GOALS AND OBJECTIVES
  A. Management Goals and Objectives
    1. Has management failed to develop a mission statement?
    2. Is the client unrealistic in assessing business strengths and weaknesses?
    3. Would specific and realistic goals for different operations or departments be helpful to management?
    4. Is management having difficulty in:
       a. Maintaining or increasing market share?
       b. Overcoming a break-even point?
       c. Penetrating new markets?
       d. Making acquisitions?
       e. Developing products?
    5. Has the client considered tax planning in connection with goals and objectives?

B. Entrepreneurial Goals and Objectives
    1. Is the owner's statement of goals and objectives vague or unrealistic?
    2. Do family relationships weaken management morale or effectiveness?
    3. Is the business tax position inappropriate because it is unduly affected by the owner's tax position?
    4. Could the IRS raise the issue of unreasonable compensation?
    5. Has the client failed to consider tax and estate planning in relation to goals and objectives?
    6. Would a valuation of company equity be desirable?

C. Short-Range, Long-Range, and Strategic Planning
    1. Do plans lack attainable or measurable goals?
    2. Are there failures to communicate plans, compare plans with results, or revise plans as appropriate?

D. Budgeting
    1. Are budgets unrealistic?
    2. Do budgets inadequately provide for control and performance measurement?
    3. Are budgets inconsistent with:
        a. Assigned responsibilities?
        b. Short-range planning?
        c. Long-range planning?
        d. Strategic planning?
    4. Does management neglect budgets in planning, comparing results, and controlling operations?
    5. Is discounted cash-flow analysis overlooked in budgeting decisions?

E. Market Share and Industry Status
    1. Does management have insufficient information for decision making about the company's:
        a. Sales-volume market share?
        b. Competitive status for products or services?

F. Markets
   1. Is there inadequate definition and monitoring of:
      a. Existing markets?
      b. Potential markets?
   2. Are marketing plans inadequate?
G. Territories and Siting
   1. Is there inadequate planning for territorial expansion for:
      a. Sales?
      b. Physical distribution?
      c. Facilities siting?
H. Profitability
   1. Is there inadequate planning for profitability by:
      a. Product or service?
      b. Sales regions?
      c. Profit centers?
   2. Is profitability planning unrealistic considering:
      a. Investment?
      b. Sales volume?
      c. Owner compensation?
I. Growth
   1. Considering sales and profitability goals, is there insufficient planning for growth in:
      a. Promotion?
      b. Production?
      c. Staffing?
      d. Facilities?
   2. Are the client's goals for growth unrealistic?
J. Continuity
   1. Has the owner expressed an interest in getting out of the business?
   2. Are there any signs of friendly or hostile takeovers?
   3. Is the compensation plan insufficient to retain key personnel?

   4. Are there insufficient plans for the succession of key officers?

   5. Is there a threat of losing substantial customers or supply sources?

K. Performance Measures

   1. Are there adverse trends or industry comparisons for these ratios:

      a. Current ratio?

      b. Quick ratio?

      c. Total debt/total assets?

      d. Net sales/total assets?

      e. Net profits/total assets?

      f. Net profits/net worth?

      g. Net profits/net sales?

      h. Days inventory?

      i. Days receivables?

      j. Net sales/employee?

II. CAPITAL AND FINANCIAL MANAGEMENT

A. Equity

   1. Are the debt-to-equity relationships unfavorable?

   2. Is planning for capital needs overlooked or unrealistic?

   3. Are there important disagreements between management and investors?

   4. Are there important failures to communicate with investors?

B. Debt

   1. Is there a mismatch in financing long-term assets with long-term debt?

   2. Are there debt covenants that hinder profitability and growth?

   3. Is debt inconsistent with ability to repay?

   4. Is there inadequate planning or provision for debt reduction?

5. Is the line of credit insufficient for short-term growth?

6. Could relations with lenders be improved?

7. Are there important failures to communicate with lenders?

8. Is the company hurt by inadequate negotiating technique in arranging debt provisions?

9. In debt-equity forecasting, are these items overlooked:

    a. Sales growth?

    b. Fixed-asset additions?

    c. Product development?

C. Fixed Assets

1. Is there a failure to analyze lease/buy/make options in fixed-asset acquisitions?

2. Is there a failure to use discounted cash-flow analysis in lease/buy decisions or in fixed-asset acquisitions?

3. Does the company fail to maintain proper schedules of fixed-asset acquisitions, retirement, and depreciation?

4. Are there inadequate approvals for asset additions or retirements?

5. Is there a failure to develop, document, or communicate policies governing capitalizing versus expensing?

D. Working Capital

1. Is working capital insufficient?

2. Is the composition of working capital inadequately structured?

3. Are there unfavorable trends in the composition of working capital?

4. Do working-capital ratios compare unfavorably with industry working-capital ratios?

5. Are present funds or borrowings insufficient for working-capital needs?

E. Cash Management

1. Is the company's method of forecasting cash requirements inadequate?

2. Is there failure in monitoring cash needs?

3. Are cash needs greater than cash flow in relation to working-capital obligations, debt repayment, and expansion?

4. Has the company overlooked sources and methods of financing such as:

    a. Lines of credit?

    b. Notes?

    c. Factoring?

    d. Leasing versus purchasing?

    e. Bonds?

5. Has the company failed to use payroll services, electronic transfers, lockboxes, and similar banking services?

6. Are accounts payable, accounts receivable, and capital budgeting overlooked in forecasting cash needs?

7. Can the company convert to cash idle assets such as:

    a. Obsolete inventory or slow-moving inventory?

    b. Unused property, plant, or equipment?

8. Are current interest rates overlooked in granting or taking cash discounts?

9. Do cash shortages result in supplier complaints or unfavorable terms?

10. Are current interest rates overlooked in reviewing compensating balances?

11. Is multilocation banking unjustified?

12. Are lines of credit inadequate?

13. Are advantages lost in the investment of excess funds?

14. Could the company alleviate a severe cash shortage by measures such as:

      a. Using temporary help rather than new hires?

      b. Using contribution analysis to eliminate marginal outlets?

      c. Giving bonuses or raises in stock rather than in cash?

15. Would direct deposit of wages in employee accounts or a draft system reduce cash-account payroll balances?

16. Is there a failure to deposit cash daily?

17. Are over-the-counter cash transactions inadequately controlled (cash-register tapes)?

18. Do individuals who prepare bank reconciliations also handle cash receipts or disbursements record keeping?

19. Is there a failure to bond individuals handling cash?

20. Are there inadequate controls over check signing?

F. Credit

1. Has the company overlooked the effects of its credit terms on profits and cash flow?

2. Is there inadequate segregation of duties between sales and credit and collections?

3. May customers or clients receive credit without satisfying explicit quantitative and qualitative credit-worthiness standards?

4. Are credit approvals delayed or erroneous because of delays in receivables processing?

5. Are credit-cutoff and collection steps vague, inappropriate, or inadequately supervised?

6. Do credit approvals delay order processing?

7. Are credit customers unaware of credit limits and credit terms?

G. Receivables

1. Does the company inadequately monitor:

      a. Trends in credit sales?

      b. Accounts receivable aging?

      c. Affects of credit limits?

2. Is receivables processing inappropriate, considering:
    a. Required credit approvals?
    b. Average value of accounts?
    c. Collection experience?
3. Have interest charges for late payments been overlooked?
4. Is there an adverse trend in bad-debt write-offs as a percentage of sales and as a percentage of receivables?
5. Is the accounts-receivable subsidiary ledger infrequently reconciled to the control ledger?
6. Are statements to customers sent too infrequently?
7. Is there inadequate management authorization of write-offs?

H. Billing
1. Are controls insufficient to prevent orders from being shipped without invoicing?
2. Is there unnecessary transcribing of information from orders to invoices?
3. Would billing be improved by one-write systems or computer processing?
4. Are billing prices, extensions, and discounts checked insufficiently or excessively, considering average value of amounts due?
5. Are there delays in mailing invoices or statements?
6. Do billing delays affect cash flow or timely inventory posting?

I. Collections
1. Has the company failed to prepare collection policies, procedures, and forms?
2. Could collections be improved through:
    a. Increasing proportionate collection effort for larger accounts?
    b. Processing high-dollar invoices first?

      c. Not paying sales commissions until receivables are collected?

      d. Cycle billing more than once a month?

      e. Sending invoices to major customers before their monthly payment cutoff?

  3. Are collection efforts inappropriately timed or escalated?

  4. Are approvals inadequate for referral to collection agencies or litigation?

J. Accounts Payable

  1. Is there a planning failure in matching peak payables with peak receipts?

  2. Are there key suppliers, without alternatives, who could interrupt business?

  3. Has an aging schedule for payables been overlooked?

  4. Would a payables due-date system assist the client in improving supplier relations or taking advantage of discounts?

  5. Are accounts payable approvals and processes inappropriate considering average amounts due, credit terms, and supplier relations?

  6. Considering the current cost of borrowing, are there failures to exploit credit terms?

  7. Are opportunities for cash discounts lost because of error or late payments?

  8. Has the company overlooked installment payments with a balloon installment to better match its own cash flow?

  9. Does the client miss critical payments to important suppliers or lenders?

 10. Are there controls or approvals that are more appropriate for purchasing than for payables?

 11. Are there oversights or errors in posting payments to the general ledger and inventory records?

 12. Does the company fail to match invoices against receiving records before approving payment?

13. Is there a failure to match purchase orders, receiving reports, and vendor invoices?

14. Is the company evasive rather than forthcoming in dealing with creditors?

III. ORGANIZATION

A. Structure

1. Would there be greater advantages to a different form of business organization such as:

   a. Sole proprietorship?

   b. Partnership?

   c. C corporation?

   d. S corporation?

2. Would mergers or consolidations with related entities be advantageous?

3. Is the board of directors inactive or inadequately prepared for its duties?

4. Is management insufficiently knowledgeable, skilled, or experienced?

B. Organization

1. Considering function, are reporting relationships inappropriate or counterproductive?

2. Is there a failure to communicate a common understanding of the company's organization?

3. Has management overlooked the:

   a. Organizational chart?

   b. Job description?

   c. Policy manual?

   d. Procedures?

4. Are committees used ineffectively or inappropriately?

5. Do committee members misunderstand their charge?

6. Is there inadequate coordination between:

   a. Production and sales?

   b. Production and purchasing?

      c. Production and personnel administration?

      d. Sales and financial management?

C. Policy

    1.   Are policies inadequately developed or communicated?

    2.   Are policies dated, or do they fail to support company goals?

D. Authority and Responsibility

    1.   Is authority inadequately matched with responsibility?

    2.   Is line responsibility versus staff or technical responsibility misunderstood?

    3.   In delegation, is there inappropriate assignment, supervision, or follow-up?

    4.   Are spans of control excessive?

    5.   Are duties inadequately understood by those responsible?

    6.   Are areas of responsibility ill defined or poorly understood?

    7.   Are individuals who are properly concerned overlooked in approval processes?

E. Staffing

    1.   Are members of management or important staff members unqualified?

    2.   Does the company lack skilled staff commensurate with its size and complexity in such areas as:

      a. Purchasing?

      b. Engineering?

      c. Personnel administration?

      d. Cost accounting?

      e. Research and development?

      f. Financial management?

    3.   Would organizational performance be improved by hiring or training a:

      a. MIS Manager?

      b. Chief financial officer?

      c. Director of purchasing?

      d. Director of personnel?

      e. Director of sales or marketing?

      f. Production manager?

      g. Controller?

      h. Internal auditor?

4. Has management failed to provide for orderly succession through assignments and training?

5. Would an inventory of management skills help in management development, succession, and planning?

6. Has staffing failed to anticipate turnover, retirements, or future needs?

7. Are workloads excessive or light in specific areas?

8. Have unfilled positions resulted in lowered performance?

F. Operating Procedures

1. Are procedures inadequately developed, reviewed, communicated, or enforced?

2. Are closely related activities divided among different decision-making authorities?

3. Is the flow of information inadequately coordinated?

4. Are procedures poorly defined or out of date?

5. Is there a failure to provide action plans where they are helpful?

G. Office Procedures

1. Are there delays, duplication, bottlenecks, or error-prone portions in office systems?

2. Do procedures manuals adequately describe office routines?

3. Would the reliability of office operations be improved through:

      a. Job rotation?

      b. Training?

     c. More versatile job descriptions?

4. Could duplication or transcription be reduced through:

     a. Multiple-part forms?

     b. One-write forms?

     c. Charge or identification plates?

5. Could efficiency be introduced by updating equipment used for:

     a. Mailing?

     b. Sorting?

     c. Reproduction?

     d. Calculating or computing?

     e. Phone communication?

6. Would cost savings result from outside versus in-house printing?

7. Could filing, information input, or information retrieval be improved through:

     a. Computers?

     b. Microfiche?

     c. Microfilm?

     d. Optical scanners?

8. Could unused files be more economically stored or destroyed?

9. Would word processors increase efficiency?

IV. MARKETING

A. Market Planning

1. Are marketing plans unrealistic considering the results of market research and analysis?

2. Has the company overlooked opportunities for growth through:

     a. Government sales?

     b. Foreign markets?

     c. Acquiring suppliers or distributors?

     d. Acquiring competitors?

3. Is management uninformed about market share or market-share potential?

4. In gathering information for market planning, does management overlook:
   a. Government publications (Statistical Abstract, etc.)?
   b. Trade associations and trade publications?
   c. Practices of competitors?
   d. Salespersons' views of customer needs and desires?

5. In market planning, has management overlooked competitive factors such as:
   a. Pricing?
   b. Geographic area or siting?
   c. Quality?
   d. Product or service development, features, and variety?
   e. Servicing and warranty?
   f. Market definition and segmentation?
   g. Promotion and distribution?

6. Does the client overlook industry statistics and data in evaluating company operations?

7. Does the company fail to analyze competitors':
   a. Pricing policies?
   b. Products and distribution?
   c. Catalogs, advertising, and promotion?
   d. Market share?

8. Has the company failed to develop an overall plan for advertising and promotion?

9. In preparing sales forecasts and reports, has the company overlooked:
   a. Sales by individual?
   b. Sales by territory?
   c. Sales by division?
   d. Sales by product?

      e. Sales by customer type?

      f. Sales by current and prior periods?

10. Have products or services been introduced without test marketing?

11. Has the company overlooked trend analysis in:

    a. Product line?

    b. Customer demographics?

    c. Market share?

12. Does the client compete with his or her own distributors by selling directly to consumers?

13. Are discounts to wholesalers insufficient to encourage aggressive selling?

B. Customers

1. Does the company fail to exploit market potential in customer mix or volume for certain types of customers?

2. Would an analysis of profitability by customer type be helpful?

3. Are prices for different customer types inconsistent with volume or profitability?

4. Has the client failed to develop a profile of its customers concerning:

    a. Price sensitivity?

    b. Demographics?

    c. Tastes?

    d. Service expected?

5. Is the company threatened by an excessively narrow customer base?

6. Are certain inventory costs unjustified in relation to the profitability of customers for that inventory?

7. Would profitability be improved by serving different customer types or market segments through different marketing routes such as:

    a. Direct sales?

    b. Agents?

       c. Distributors?

       d. Commission sales?

       e. Franchising?

       f. Manufacturer's representatives?

    8. Would a change in customer mix improve profitability?

C. Products and Product Planning

    1. Could product mix be improved to match the market?

    2. Are there opportunities to improve profitability by changing the product line?

    3. Has the company failed to research or to analyze:

       a. Profitability by product?

       b. Sales cost by product?

       c. Sales volume by product?

       d. Inventory by product?

       e. Product quality or improvement?

       f. Product packaging?

    4. Are there discontinued products in inventory?

    5. Could low-volume or unprofitable products be discontinued?

    6. Is research and development inadequately monitored?

    7. Is the research and development budget inadequate?

    8. Should the company be considering new or alternative products?

    9. Has the company neglected sources (customers, suppliers, salespersons, distributors, etc.) in gathering ideas for new or modified products or packaging?

    10. In designing new products, has the client overlooked:

       a. Customer complaints, comments, or desires?

       b. Market research?

       c. Competitive products?

      d. Production costs?

      e. Distribution?

11. Are design specifications insufficiently detailed?

12. Are there cost-producing and superfluous design features?

13. Are new product prototypes inadequately tested for:

      a. Function?

      b. Reliability?

      c. Safety?

      d. Repairability?

      e. Customer appeal?

14. Is there insufficient test marketing of new products?

15. Could a new product fill slow periods in production or sales?

16. If the client is a wholesaler or distributor, does the client overlook:

      a. Seasonally adjusted product mix?

      b. Shortened response time to market demand?

      c. Changes in customer demographics?

D. Pricing

1. Are pricing policies poorly defined, communicated, monitored, or followed?

2. Do those who make pricing decisions have insufficient authority, responsibility, knowledge, or experience?

3. Have pricing policies overlooked:

      a. Direct costs and overhead?

      b. Discounts, rebates, and allowances?

      c. Cost of extending credit?

      e. Freight and shipping costs?

      f. Inflation?

      g. Sales commissions?

4. Would an analysis of the relationships between price, volume, and profitability be helpful?

5. Is pricing structure unreasonable or inconsistent considering:
   a. Competition?
   b. Market conditions?
   c. Quality?
   d. Packaging for market segmentation?
   e. Industry practices?
   f. Actual costs?
   g. Legal or regulatory requirements?

6. Is there failure to study competitors prices when bids are lost?

7. Are bids or prices too high or too low because of inadequate cost information?

8. Are customers or clients given inconsistent or irregular prices?

9. Are trade discounts inconsistently administered?

10. Do trade discounts depart from industry norms?

11. Are discounts inconsistent with actual savings due to larger orders?

12. Are initial gross markups sufficient to provide planned gross margin after markdowns?

13. Are markups and markdowns inadequately recorded?

14. Is there insufficient control over markdowns for shopworn or damaged stock?

15. Do sales records fail to highlight slow-moving stock?

16. Do inventory records permit the purchase of additional slow-moving stock?

17. Is the inventory system sluggish in accommodating rapid changes in sales volume?

E. Promotion and Advertising
   1. Is there a failure to accomplish specific goals through advertising and promotion such as:

       a. Promoting benefit, features, or price?

       b. Fostering name or product recognition?

       c. Motivating salespersons?

  2. Are advertising and promotion undifferentiated in targeting:

       a. Final consumer?

       b. Retailer?

       c. Distributor?

  3. Are advertising and promotion media improperly matched to specific markets or uncoordinated in using:

       a. Contests?

       b. Coupons?

       c. Direct mail?

       d. Displays?

       e. Trade shows?

       f. Free samples?

       g. Phone campaigns?

       h. Radio advertising?

       i. Space advertising?

       j. Television advertising?

  4. Would public relations consulting assist the client?

F. Retailing

  1. In measuring gross profit, does the client overlook markup by:

       a. Item?

       b. Category?

       c. Department?

  2. Is the client ineffective in getting the greatest benefit from suppliers considering:

       a. Price, allowances, discounts, and rebates?

       b. Inventory service, returns, and consignments?

       c. Delivery, quality, and guarantees?

3. In determining the items to carry, does the client overlook:

   a. Price, quality, or competition?

   b. Prior sales, profitability, or customer tastes?

4. Is the client's stock improperly balanced between high-volume/low-markup items and low-volume/high-markup items?

5. Does the client suffer stock-outs for high-volume items?

6. Are sales of low-turnover items poorly timed, planned, or located for maximum traffic exposure?

7. In controlling markdowns, does the client fail to maintain schedules or provide adequate supervision?

8. Does the client neglect experimentation with new merchandise?

9. In organizing and displaying merchandise, does the client overlook:

   a. Item category grouping?

   b. Price grouping?

   c. Customer age or sex grouping?

   d. Associated merchandise?

   e. Display assistance by suppliers?

10. Are controls for inventory shrinkage inadequate?

G. Sales Force

1. Do sales managers handle major accounts while neglecting to supervise, train, or support the sales force?

2. Are procedures for assigning customers, product lines, or territories unfair or ineffective?

3. Are salespersons confused about their priorities in:

   a. Soliciting and writing up orders?

   b. Handling complaints and servicing accounts?

   c. Providing technical help to customers?

       d. Developing new customers?

       e. Promoting specific products?

    4. Is there a failure to reinforce standards of performance by appropriate compensation or incentive arrangements?

    5. Is the sales force too small to serve the assigned geographic area?

    6. Are call reports inadequately summarized and reviewed?

    7. Do sales analyses and reports inadequately identify problems, shortfalls, or changes in customer buying behavior?

    8. Does sales training overlook:

       a. Sales technique?

       b. Product knowledge?

       c. Customer or client knowledge?

       d. Company policies and procedures?

    9. Is the selling effort insufficiently supported by:

       a. Brochures, catalogs, and price lists?

       b. Samples or demonstration materials?

   10. Are sales leads, cold calls, and new customer contact inadequately encouraged, supported, or monitored?

   11. Is sales-force turnover excessive?

H. Selling Costs

    1. Would it be helpful to analyze selling costs by:

       a. Product?

       b. Customer?

       c. Territory?

       d. Salesperson?

    2. Is there a failure to compare budgeted and actual selling costs?

    3. Does company overlook measurements of sales productivity such as:

       a. Sales cost per sales?

       b. Sales cost per transaction?

  c. Sales per salesperson?

 4. Is sales staffing ineffectively matched with periods of high sales volume?

 5. Is there a failure to communicate clear polices and procedures for sales expense accounts?

I. Order Processing

 1. Do skilled salespersons spend significant time taking orders when this could be done by someone else?

 2. Could clerical staff be used more effectively in taking orders?

 3. Are salespersons' orders or phone orders lost because of ineffective or inefficient order taking?

 4. Do individuals taking orders have insufficient information concerning:

  a. Prices and discounts?

  b. Customer or client knowledge?

  c. Customer or client credit standing?

  d. Inventories and shipping schedules?

  e. Add-ons, related products, or alternatives to stock-outs?

 5. Are there errors or delays caused by the transcribing of data when taking orders?

 6. Are customer complaints and order cancellations handled too slowly or ineffectively?

 7. Have orders been lost or delayed due to:

  a. Inadequate staffing for top demands?

  b. Poor match of work hours and ordering times?

  c. Delays in phone or mail communications?

  d. Erroneous shipping information?

  e. Redundant or excessive approvals?

 8. Are there significant errors in:

  a. Writing orders?

  b. Pricing?

  c. Fulfilling orders?

  d. Shipping quantities?

      e. Shipping destinations?

      f. Freight charges?

      g. Adjusting inventory records?

    9. Are there significant lost shipments or returned goods?

   10. Are there inadequate gross checks on the value of sales in comparison to the value of orders shipped?

   11. Do errors occur in order assembly due to:

      a. Illegible orders or poorly labeled stock?

      b. Untrained workers?

      c. Poorly organized stock?

      d. Inefficient work flow or traffic flow?

J. Servicing

   1. Does the client use the most effective system of product servicing such as:

      a. Client-owned service centers?

      b. Independent service centers?

   2. Are there significant customer complaints about service?

   3. Are customer services inadequate in the areas of:

      a. Repair?

      b. Operating instructions and support?

      c. Installation?

   4. Are customer services inconsistent with pricing, product, or industry practices?

   5. Are service personnel insufficiently trained?

   6. Is feedback from service personnel neglected in product design?

V. PRODUCTION AND SERVICES

A. Planning and Control

   1. Is discounted cash-flow analysis overlooked in capital expenditures for plant and machinery?

   2. Is production inadequately based on sales forecasting?

3. Is production forecasting overlooked?

4. Are delivery dates missed because of poor scheduling?

5. Are production runs ineffectively tracked or timed?

6. Does production scheduling provide unreliable dates for materials requirements and production run completion?

7. In scheduling production, does the company overlook:

   a. Just-in-time inventory scheduling?

   b. Economic order quantity?

   c. Response to market demand?

   d. Traffic control?

   e. Materials?

   f. Machinery capacity?

   g. Labor availability?

   h. Most efficient production run size?

B. Purchasing

1. Are there failures to conduct purchasing according to policies and procedures?

2. Is the purchase approval process inadequately documented or followed?

3. Are ultimate users inadequately represented in purchasing decisions?

4. Are purchase requisitions and purchase orders inappropriate considering needs and system requirements?

5. Are those involved in purchasing inadequately trained or experienced in:

   a. Value analysis?

   b. Specifications?

   c. Negotiating skills?

   d. Industry practices?

   e. Market trends?

6. Are those involved in purchasing also responsible for paying bills or receiving?

7. In purchase decisions, does the company overlook:
    a. Quality?
    b. Delivery requirements?
    c. Warranties?
    d. Reliability?
    e. Supplier technical support?
    f. Lead time?
    g. Safety stock levels?

8. Do supervision, budgets, policies, and procedures inadequately control:
    a. Emergency purchases?
    b. Complicated purchases?
    c. Small purchases?
    d. Blanket or open-to-buy purchases?

9. When raw materials are commodities, are futures markets overlooked or used ineffectively to protect planned purchases?

10. Is there a failure to use prenumbered purchase orders?

11. Is there inadequate segregation of duties between personnel in purchasing, receiving, and bookkeeping?

12. Are there failures to compare suppliers' monthly statements and recorded payables?

C. Supplier Relations

1. In selecting suppliers, has financial ratio analysis of suppliers been overlooked?

2. Is there critical dependence on a few suppliers?

3. Are suppliers unduly influencing buying decisions?

4. Are periodic reviews of vendor performance and long-standing supplier relationships overlooked?

5. Is supplier support inadequate regarding:

       a. Technical updates?

       b. Training?

       c. Spare parts?

       d. Advertising and promotions?

       e. Promotional and technical literature?

  6. Do suppliers fail to inform buyers of planned price increases or service changes?

  7. Are gifts accepted from suppliers?

D. Receiving

  1. Are receiving procedures and records ineffectively integrated with the inventory system and the accounts payable system?

  2. Would efficiency be improved if receiving documents were prepared along with purchase orders?

  3. Is security inadequate in receiving areas?

  4. Are there failures to:

       a. Check for damage?

       b. Check for complete shipment?

       c. Check for weight when appropriate?

       d. Check item count when appropriate?

       e. Document incoming goods on receiving reports?

  5. Are there delays in notifying purchasing of incomplete or damaged shipments?

  6. Are incoming packages inadequately identified by labels or stamps?

  7. Do receivers have insufficient information to route incoming shipments and returned goods?

E. Inventory Management

  1. Does management fail to consider inventory as an investment to be compared to other types of capital investment?

  2. Are there opportunities to computerize the inventory system?

3. Is the inventory system inadequately integrated with:
   a. Sales forecasting?
   b. Production?
   c. Customer demand?
   d. Purchasing?
   e. Receiving and shipping?
4. Is there a failure to calculate and monitor inventory turnover?
5. Are perpetual-inventory records out of date or inaccurate?
6. Are physical-inventory results out of balance with inventory records?
7. Are reorder points incorrectly triggered by inventory records?
8. Are service levels incorrectly set, or are excessive sales lost due to stock outages?
9. Are reorder lead times too short or too long?
10. Has economic-order-quantity purchasing been overlooked?
11. Are inventory carrying costs overlooked?
12. Would ABC inventory classification help the company?
13. Is obsolete or damaged inventory incorrectly valued?
14. Is inventory custody inadequately segregated from shipping and receiving?
15. Is inventory inadequately protected?

F. Manufacturing
   1. Would a review of production processes or systems by qualified engineers assist the client?
   2. Has the client failed to determine optimum manufacturing runs or the economic manufacturing quantity?
   3. Has the client failed to solicit suggestions or overlooked suggestions for production improvement from:

    a. Suppliers?

    b. Operators?

    c. Supervisors?

    d. Equipment manufacturers?

    e. Engineers?

4. Has the client overlooked steps to:

    a. Cut setup time?

    b. Reduce materials handling?

    c. Improve work design?

    d. Reduce physical effort?

    e. Improve traffic flow or workstation arrangements?

    f. Reduce waste or scrap?

    g. Measure production?

    h. Eliminate bottlenecks?

G. Quality Control

1. Are there important failures to monitor and analyze the quality of:

    a. Raw materials?

    b. Work in process?

    c. Finished goods?

2. Are there many customer complaints regarding quality?

3. Are there failures to monitor, investigate, and resolve complaints?

4. Is packaging or type of carrier the cause of damage and quality complaints?

5. Have relationships between design, engineering, and manufacturing process been overlooked in studying quality control?

6. Are quality controls obsolete or ineffective considering current technology, systems, and product standards?

7. Are rejection rates high?

8. Is rework of goods excessive?

9. Would training programs for supervisors and employees foster improved quality?

H. Supervision

1. Do supervisors have inadequate skills to guide, motivate, and instruct subordinates?

2. Is supervisory responsibility incorrectly matched with authority?

3. Are there an insufficient number of supervisors?

4. Are supervisors too involved in operations to delegate and supervise the work of others?

5. Does management provide insufficient support or training for supervisors?

I. Manufacturing and Labor Cost Control

1. Does the company overlook controls such as:

   a. Cost accounting?

   b. Cost centers?

   c. Budgets and variance analysis?

   d. Capacity utilization?

   e. Labor utilization?

   f. Cost/volume/efficiency/price analysis?

   g. Scrap reports?

   h. Reject reports?

   i. Downtime analysis?

2. Is production data neglected in preparing estimates?

3. Are production standards out of date?

4. Is there a failure to compare production standards with labor costs and analyze variances?

5. Are there failures to document production runs, repair work, and maintenance work through work orders?

6. Are there false production counts?

7. Are production counts out of balance with inventory counts or piecework counts?

8. Are dated or unverified average production rates used for estimates, pricing, or pay?

      9. Are there inadequate incentives to maintain quality and reduce rejects?

    10. Is overhead allocated on an unreasonable basis?

J. Warehousing

    1. Could warehouse siting be significantly improved considering:

       a. Customer locations?

       b. Transportation facilities?

       c. Supplier locations?

       d. Production facilities?

    2. Is warehouse space insufficient or excessive?

    3. Is there inadequate warehouse provision for:

       a. Traffic flow?

       b. Flexible space usage?

       c. Vertical space usage?

       d. Access to high-volume items?

       e. Item labeling and containers?

       f. Physical inventory?

       g. Fire protection?

       h. Lighting?

       i. Maintenance and cleaning?

       j. Security?

       k. Insurance?

K. Shipping

    1. Has the client failed to record and analyze transportation costs?

    2. Would a study of comparative transportation costs help the client?

    3. Are minimum shipment size, shipment schedules, and delivery schedules inefficient or uneconomical?

    4. Has the client overlooked options for reducing transportation costs such as:

       a. Rescheduling to reduce demurrage?

       b. Different packaging to reduce dunnage?

   c. Safer transportation to reduce packaging costs?

   d. Improved packaging to reduce transportation costs?

   e. Product redesign to reduce transportation or packaging costs?

   f. Increased distribution centers to reduce shipping costs?

5. Could shipping costs be lowered through consolidations for carload, truckload, or containerized lots?

6. Are there excessive complaints from customers due to:

   a. Damaged shipments?

   b. Delayed shipments?

   c. Back orders?

   d. Partial shipments?

7. Do frequent stock-outs require split shipments?

8. Are shipments delayed to avoid split shipments?

9. Are claims for damaged shipments ineffectively pursued?

10. Are facilities inefficiently arranged for shipping?

11. Would efficiency be improved by the use of updated or additional equipment such as:

   a. Forklifts?

   b. Pallets?

12. Are there failures to coordinate shipping and transportation schedules?

13. Are so many shipments marked "RUSH" that the term is ignored?

14. Is there a failure to count and record shipments when shipments are loaded?

15. Are sample checks of shipment counts overlooked?

16. Where client company has its own trucking fleet, could efficiency or economy be improved by:

   a. Vehicle maintenance programs?

      b. Driver training?

      c. Accident prevention and reporting program?

      d. Review and renegotiation of insurance?

      e. Vehicle additions or replacement?

      f. Computerized vehicle routing?

      g. Tractors?

L. Facilities and Machinery

  1. Is the plant and equipment inadequately:

      a. Maintained?

      b. Updated?

      c. Utilized?

  2. Is there inadequate analysis of make/rent/buy options?

  3. Are schedules of fixed-asset additions, depreciation, and retirements inadequately maintained?

  4. Are maintenance records overlooked in new machinery purchases?

  5. Is there a failure to minimize downtime through scheduled preventive maintenance?

  6. Is the plant or workplace cluttered or disorganized?

  7. In controlling maintenance costs, does the client overlook:

      a. Budgets?

      b. Work orders?

      c. Competitive bids?

  8. Is spare-parts availability a problem?

  9. Is there excessive overtime for maintenance and repair personnel?

  10. Are files inadequately maintained for:

      a. Machinery warranties?

      b. Repair and operating manuals?

      c. Parts lists and reorder sources?

      d. Blueprints?

VI. HUMAN RESOURCES

A. Workforce Planning and Utilization

1. Has workforce planning overlooked future personnel requirements by:
   a. Job description?
   b. Job classification?
   c. Function or department?
   d. Managerial, administrative, supervisory, or production levels?
2. Has workforce planning failed to specify:
   a. Numbers of new hires for each function?
   b. Sources of new hires for each function?
   c. Timing of new hires for each function?

B. Personnel Administration

1. Is there a need for additional personnel in:
   a. Management?
   b. Production?
   c. Sales?
   d. Administration?
2. Is there inadequate statistical information on:
   a. Turnover?
   b. Employment offers/hires?
   c. Employment applications/hires?
   d. Absenteeism?
3. Are performance standards and job descriptions inadequately documented?
4. Are personnel records out of date or incomplete?
5. Do employee personnel records fail to include:
   a. Experience, work, training, and academic history?
   b. Marital and family status and emergency contacts?
   c. Skills and evaluations?
6. Is employee morale unsatisfactory?
7. Are exit interviews overlooked?

C. Communications
   1. Is upward or downward communication unsatisfactory?
   2. Does management fail to communicate company goals and accomplishments to employees?
   3. Do communications overlook any important segment of the company?
   4. Has the company failed to solicit suggestions from:
      a. Employees?
      b. Customers?
      c. Suppliers?
      d. Owners or investors?
      e. Regulators?
   5. Are company house organs or newsletters ineffective in communicating or building goodwill?
D. Recruiting and Hiring
   1. Are interviewing practices unacceptable or discriminatory?
   2. Are those responsible for recruiting and hiring unaware of government regulation and legal liability in this area?
   3. Is there a failure to document or follow hiring policies?
   4. In recruiting, has the company overlooked:
      a. Colleges and universities?
      b. Referrals from present employees?
      c. Trade publications?
      d. Placement services?
   5. Are appropriate interviews, screening, and reference checks overlooked for new hires?
   6. Are employment requirements and testing unrelated to job performance or discriminatory?
   7. Are employee manuals out-of-date, incomplete, or inaccurate?

8. Is there a failure to document, understand, or follow antidiscrimination policies?

9. Would a probationary period with performance reviews improve performance and reduce turnover?

E. Training

1. Is orientation overlooked for new employees?

2. Is on-the-job training inadequately supervised?

3. Does the company overlook alternatives to training such as:

   a. Changing policies or procedures?

   b. Providing closer supervision?

   c. Hiring more experienced personnel?

4. Do performance reviews suggest the need for additional training?

5. Would the company be helped by a survey of training needs for:

   a. Production or service personnel?

   b. Administrative personnel?

   c. Management?

6. Do company training programs fail to specify skills outcomes?

7. Is government-sponsored training or tax credits for training overlooked?

8. Are trade association and industry-sponsored training overlooked?

9. Would procedures or operating manuals assist training?

F. Safety

1. Is there a failure to collect, record, and analyze safety data?

2. Are accidents increasing?

3. Has management failed to determine the costs of accidents?

4. Have these causal factors been overlooked?

   a. New hires or inexperience?

      b. Inadequate training?

      c. Poor supervision?

      d. Unsatisfactory safety equipment, devices, or clothing?

      e. Inadequate or unenforced safety rules?

      f. Low morale?

      g. Undue pressure for production?

  5. Are dangerous or poisonous materials improperly labeled or stored?

  6. Have there been OSHA inspections, reports violations, or warnings?

  7. Would a program for accident prevention help the client?

G. Compensation and Benefits

  1. Has a formal, documented program of compensation administration been overlooked?

  2. As a basis for compensation administration, has the company overlooked:

      a. Job descriptions?

      b. Comparative job rating?

      c. Wage surveys?

      d. Salary ranges?

  3. Is compensation insufficiently competitive?

  4. Are there compensation complaints due to:

      a. Comparative pay scales within the company?

      b. Comparative industry pay scales?

      c. Regional pay scales?

      d. Lack of merit or experience pay increases?

  5. Are regular compensation reviews overlooked?

  6. If there is incentive compensation, does it:

      a. Fail to produce the desired performance?

      b. Lead to complaints and misunderstandings?

      c. Achieve short-term goals at the expense of long-term goals?

7. Has the client failed to review benefits programs to assure they accord with the growth or reduction of the company?

8. Are benefits inadequate as compared to the industry or region?

9. Would the client be helped by benefits programs such as:

   a. Profit sharing?

   b. Pensions?

   c. 401K or deferred compensation?

   d. Keogh?

   e. Educational assistance?

   f. Day care or dependent care?

   g. Stock options?

   h. Cafeteria plan?

10. Has tax planning been overlooked in structuring benefits?

11. Does the client unsatisfactorily administer health, HMO, or insurance programs such as:

    a. Officers life insurance?

    b. Group life insurance?

    c. Group health insurance?

    d. Major medical insurance?

    e. Disability and accident insurance?

    f. Health Maintenance Organization?

    g. Internal health care or health maintenance facilities?

12. Does the client fail to analyze insurance rate increases to see if they are justified by claims experience?

H. Evaluation

   1. Has the company overlooked a formal plan for regular employee evaluation?

   2. Are performance standards and evaluation criteria inadequately described or communicated?

   3. Are evaluation results inadequately documented?

4. Are the results of employee evaluations overlooked in:

    a. Compensation adjustments?

    b. Promotions?

    c. Training assignments?

5. Is there a failure to involve participants in evaluation and goal setting?

6. Are performance goals unrealistic or poorly monitored?

7. Does management fail to recognize and acknowledge exceptional performance?

I. Law and Regulations

1. For the personnel function, are there failures to:

    a. Document policies and procedures?

    b. Communicate policies and procedures?

    c. Enforce policies and procedures?

2. Do the company's personnel policies or procedures violate:

    a. The Fair Labor Standards Act?

    b. NLRB regulations?

    c. OSHA regulations?

    d. State or local regulations or legislation?

3. Do termination procedures inadequately reduce liability exposure?

J. Unions.

1. Does the company have poor relations with either internal or external bargaining groups?

2. Is the company's internal or external counsel inadequate for:

    a. Grievance settlements?

    b. Contract negotiations?

    c. Labor relations improvement?

3. Is there a failure to resolve grievances reasonably or promptly?

4. Are grievances and their resolution inadequately documented?

5. Considering industry conditions, are there frequent work stoppages, strikes, or absenteeism?

6. Are violations of work rules or poor performance inadequately documented?

7. Are supervisors insufficiently knowledgeable in dealing with industrial-relations problems?

VII. MANAGEMENT INFORMATION AND CONTROLS

A. General Ledger System

1. Is the chart of accounts too detailed or insufficiently detailed?

2. Is the system inadequately computerized?

3. Does the system fail to reflect the client's industry or particular needs?

B. Financial Statements

1. Is the system inadequate in providing financial statements and comparisons for:

a. Prior years or periods?

b. Budgets?

c. Divisions?

d. Product lines?

C. Management Information Systems

1. Is direction of the management information system inadequate regarding:

a. Needs identification?

b. Documented specifications?

c. Review and update?

2. Is there inadequate reporting and comparison of financial, operating and industry ratios?

3. Has the client overlooked:

a. Cost accounting?

b. Break-even calculations?

c. Return on investment calculations?

d. Cash-flow reports?

e. Variance and exception reports?

f. Sales trends and market share?

g. Exception reports with variable selection criteria?

h. Comparisons of current data with prior periods, standards, forecasts, and budgets?

4. Is the management information system unduly limited to accounting data?

5. Would graphics displays in reports assist management?

6. Are reports too detailed, lengthy, or insufficiently detailed?

7. Are reports inaccurate or not timely?

8. Would on-line reports assist some management functions?

9. Are there failures to route reports to those who need them?

10. Are reports inadequately adapted to management level or special function?

11. Do users have inadequate influence over report design and content?

12. Are reports insufficiently focused as a basis for action or decision making?

13. Is there failure to correct or edit input data close to the source?

D. Electronic Data Processing

1. Are there inadequate controls for:

a. Data entry?

b. Data edit or modification?

c. File protection and security?

d. Program documentation?

e. Segregation of duties?

2. Are EDP functions inadequately segregated from user departments?

3. May the EDP department initiate or authorize transactions?

4. Are functions within the EDP department inadequately segregated?

5. Are user departments insufficiently involved in systems design?

6. Are systems specifications inadequately documented or reviewed for approval?

7. Are new systems inadequately tested and approved?

8. Can unauthorized changes be made in master or transaction files?

9. Is there a failure to exploit control features of hardware or operating systems?

10. Are changes to the operating system inadequately documented or approved?

11. Is program documentation unavailable to those who need it to perform their duties?

12. Is access to data files available to those other than processing personnel?

13. Can individuals other than authorized operators access computer hardware?

14. Are there inadequate controls over the correction of errors and transactions?

15. Are there failures to use and reconcile control or batch totals at appropriate points in processing?

16. Are comparisons of output to input documents neglected?

Appendix B

BUSINESS ADVISORY COMMENT CHECKLIST

This checklist is a guide to evaluating and revising business advisory comments. "Yes" indicates the comment meets the guideline. "No" indicates a possible fault in the comment.

Content

	Yes	No
1. Does the business advisory comment include:		
Symptoms?	___	___
Problem?	___	___
Solution (recommendation)?	___	___
Benefits?	___	___
2. Does each part include client-specific detail?	___	___
3. Is the description of the problem quantified where possible?	___	___
4. Are risks, costs, and disadvantages of the solution described?	___	___
5. Have you considered possible new problems due to the solution?	___	___
6. Is the solution consistent with client priorities and goals?	___	___
7. Have benefits been quantified with appropriate qualification?	___	___
8. Do headings and subheadings emphasize benefits?	___	___
9. Is the advisory comment content and style consistent with the client corporate culture?	___	___
10. Are possible engagements described in advisory comments?	___	___

11. Have client sources been recognized and
    credited in the advisory comment?   _____ _____
12. Has the priority or importance of the
    advisory comment been evaluated?   _____ _____
13. Has the advisory comment been reviewed
    with a responsible member of management?   _____ _____

Form

14. Does the advisory comment comply with
    these readability guidelines:

    Short words?   _____ _____
    Short sentences?   _____ _____
    Active voice?   _____ _____
    Unnecessary words deleted?   _____ _____
    Client-centered instead of auditor-centered? _____ _____
15. Has the advisory comment been edited and
    proofread for:

    Sense and meaning?   _____ _____
    Word usage?   _____ _____
    Spelling, grammar, punctuation?   _____ _____
    Headings, paragraphing, bullets, white
    space?   _____ _____
    Names, titles, captions, cross-references?   _____ _____
    Tables and graphs?   _____ _____

Index

Other books of interest to you from Irwin Professional Publishing...

MARKETING TO THE AFFLUENT

Thomas J. Stanley

This premier guide reveals an accurate picture of who the affluent are, in terms of demographics, psychographics, buying, and patronage habits. The guide also includes in-depth interviews with some of the nation's top sales and marketing professionals who have successfully identified affluent prospects.
ISBN: 1-55623-105-9

EVENT-DRIVEN BUSINESS SOLUTIONS
Today's Revolution in Business and Information Technology

Eric L. Denna, J. Owen Cherrington, David P. Andros, and Anita Sawyer Hollander

This breakthrough book revolutionizes traditional thinking about business functions by encouraging companies to focus less on processes and more on defining the impact of every business event. The reader will discover how to use that information to develop new and better ways to do battle in today's economic world.
ISBN: 1-55623-942-4

ACCOUNTING
An International Perspective

Gerhard G. Mueller, Helen Gernon, and Gary Meek

This guide gives busy accountants, attorneys, and business executives the gen eral, nontechnical overview of international accounting they need to interpret information and make informed decisions. Readers will learn the key issues of international accounting, international financial statement analysis and managerial accounting.
ISBN: 0-7863-0007-8

IMPLEMENTING ACTIVITY-BASED COST MANAGEMENT
Moving From Analysis to Action

Robin Cooper

This book analyzes the experiences of eight real-life companies that took on the challenge of implementing an ABC system, revealing the mistakes, successes, and ultimate triumphs that resulted in each case. This collection of case studies helps managers understand the real value of ABC, learn to identify good design decisions in relation to their own organizational dynamics, and realize the importance of taking action based on the insights gained through ABC analysis.
ISBN: 0-86641-206-9

Available in fine bookstores and libraries everywhere!